D1606378

THE SUPERNATURAL SELF

MOSHE SHALOM

Moshe Shalom

DEDICATION

*I would like to dedicate the following book in honor of my
younger siblings, Jack, Eve, Daniel, and Sophia Shalom. I
wish you all the best in life as you all progress into adulthood,
and I hope to watch you all become your supernatural selves.*

*I would also like to dedicate this book in honor of my father
and my mother, Eliot and Galit Shalom. Anything written in
this book is a direct product of your teachings, and I thank you
for teaching me the importance of always striving to be above
what is expected, above human nature.*

Moshe Shalom

CONTEXT

Moshe Shalom

Moshe Shalom

INTRODUCTION

Human nature- it's the imperfection of humanity, the excuse we use when we fault, and the reason we disagree. It is the reason we fall to desire, the reason we judge others, and the reason we are selfish beings. What if I told you that human nature is optional? What if I told you that human nature is just a standard, but you don't have to be standard- that it is the level of the average person, but that you have the potential of being above average? This book comes to illustrate exactly that. Human nature is the challenge humanity is meant to overcome, not a law it must abide by.

The inspiration from this book comes from the 13 characteristics attributed to God in the Bible. I would like to mention here that while this text has a religious basis, it is by no means intended to be one of a religious nature. I would also like to mention that I am not a religious leader, nor scholar of any sorts, and by no means do I intend on giving any factual explanation or commentaries on religious texts. At the end of this introduction you can find an interpretation of the 13 characteristics, as well as the extrapolations I had made for them (shown is one interpretation of many, as there are many different interpretations of what the 13 characteristics are and what they entail).

For the purposes of this text, we will examine 13 principles which make up human nature, and describe how one can overcome them and become their supernatural self, their potential to be above human nature, above average and exceeding expectations. We will also examine the psychological and logical principles behind each one, and how they hinder and enhance our abilities to rise above human nature.

I want to use this time to give a piece of advice to those who continue reading forward. Reading the words on the pages of this book is a great start to overcome human nature, however it will only get you so far. In order to make the most of this book, I urge you to pace your reading with your perseverance to improve and make the most of your life. After every chapter, take a piece of paper and write down how you think the chapter you had just read can be applied to your daily life. Spend some time using the context of the chapter to change your lifestyle and habits of human nature, and once you feel you have mastered the skills you have learned thus far, you can continue reading forward.

I wish you the best of luck on your journey

towards your supernatural self, and if you must gain only one piece of knowledge from this book, let it be that you have potential, and you are in control of what others think control you.

Words of the Bible	Interpretation	Extrapolation, Chapter Topics
"God" (first time)	God has compassion before man sins	Learn from your failures. Before anyone can move on from your mistakes, you must move forward yourself
"God" (second time)	God has compassion after man sins	When somebody else causes you misfortune, grow from it and don't let the event harm you post facto
"Lord"	God has compassion to give all creatures as they need	Show kindness to all, especially when it is not expected
"Compassion"	God has mercy for humans	Forgive those who you are angry with
"Gracious"	God is gracious to people in destress	Be a leader, the distress of those around you is your distress, and their success is yours.
"Slow to anger"	God does not rush to anger, and gives humanity a chance to repent	Do not let your emotions get the best of you- rise above them
"Abundant in grace/goodness"	God has an abundance in positivity for humanity	Judge carefully, don't let judgement get a hold of you.
"Truth"	God is true, and only true	Be honest and transparent with yourself
"Provides goodness to thousands"	God provides kindness to all	Be grateful for everything you have, especially your time
"Forgives iniquity"	God forgives sin that stems from immoral acts	Respect all, because people are equal and should be treated as such
"Forgives transgression"	God forgives acts that are against Biblical law	Be mindful of how you react towards the world, and be in control of your reactions
"Forgives sins"	God forgives sin that was unintentional	Take a hold of your desires
"Cleans sins"	God will forgive all past sins once a person repents and improves	Be above the limitations of time

Chapter 1: Failing Successfully

"Falling down is not a failure. Failure comes when you stay where you have fallen." ~Socrates

Life is a bumpy car ride. The ride is rough, the kids are screaming at each other in the back, and the cars behind you are honking at you like there's no tomorrow. After several hours of driving, you feel restless. At this point, you, as the driver, have several options. You can pull over to the side of the road, walk out of the car, and walk away; walk away from the road, walk away from the noise, walk away from your problems. If you do this, you'll be giving up, never to reach the destination you drove tirelessly to reach. Another option you have is to get frustrated, and start yelling. You scare the kids and make them cry, honk at the cars in front of you, and perpetuate your troubles onto others. On top of that, you also will arrive at your destination, after so many hours of driving, cranky and upset. If that's the case, was the ride worth the struggle? Lastly, you can take control of the situation. You can play car games with the kids, play some music on the radio, and enjoy the ride. Take control of the situation- instead of getting angry at the honking cars, learn to be more patient from them. Instead of screaming at the kids for fighting, test different methods of calming them for future use.

The most common misconception of society's hard workers is that failure is the opposite of success. For as long as the concept of success has been around, people gave everything but success a negative connotation, and that has led to what we now perceive as "failure." If you look at a thesaurus, some synonyms attributed to the word failure are collapse, breakdown, and loss. Dictionaries even define the word failure as "an insufficiency," or "proving unsuccessful." (Dictionary.com)

The truth is, failure is not a deviation from the path towards success, rather it is a perpetuation towards it. As Winston Churchill once said, "Success consists of going from failure to failure without loss of enthusiasm." By attempting, and ultimately not succeeding, to reach your goal by one course of action, you learn what needs to be adjusted before you try again. Imagine you're new to archery, and pick up a bow and arrow for the first time. The first time you try shooting at a target, your arrow will likely not even come near the bulls-eye. You learn where your faults lie, adjust yourself a bit, and try again. The second time around, you use your experience of the failed attempt in order to aim for your goal a little more accurately. You may "fail" again, but all that means is that there are more adjustments that need to be made before your next attempt. Either way, you still end up closer to attaining your goal than you were when you first began.

Now that we've established that failure is not the opposite of success, all that needs to be answered is how does one rid themselves of the negative attributions of failure? In simpler terms, how does a person succeed in learning from his or her mistakes rather than stressing over them and letting them bring them down? The answer lies in one word: attitude.

In psychology, attitude is defined as a person's evaluation of an object, person, event, etc. The key word in the above definition is evaluation; when a person meets someone for the first time, they form beliefs about them from mere observation, sucking up any observational facts that he can attain from his or her surroundings. From these observations, the person forms an evaluation, or an attitude, towards that person. The same applies to objects, events, and, for the focus of this chapter, "failures." This means that when a person fails at a task, what really makes up their ability to learn and grow from it is how they evaluate the attempt, and how they shape their own attitude towards failure.

Shaping attitudes can apply to simply modifying how you react to one failed task, or to changing your attitude towards failure in general. Shaping attitudes takes time and practice, and isn't something that can happen overnight- it takes continuous effort and deliberation.

The first step in shaping one's attitude towards failure is recognizing that failure is a part of nature. Nobody is immune to messing up here and there, and there's nothing wrong with it too. The worst thing a person can do in regards to accepting their failures is believing that failure is a trait exclusive to them, that they are the only ones who bring failure. This mentality will ultimately lead the person to believe that their best option would be to turn around and quit. This one belief can hold a person back from striving for success and achieving their goals. You must truly believe that failure is a stepping stool that everybody takes in order to reach success, and that no one has ever become successful without at least one failure. This also makes sense, because we associate the word failure with struggle. Have you ever heard somebody being praised as being successful for winning the lottery? On the other hand, nobody would argue that somebody who began as a simple salesman at a company and eventually grew to become the company's CEO is not successful.

Some of the most influential people throughout history have been acquainted with failure more than once, but what led them to success is their understanding that whatever happens along the way, it's up to them to continue working and to not let it bring them down. Sylvester Stallone, the world-renown actor and screenwriter, at one point was a homeless man, struggling actor, and even needed to sell his dog for a mere $25.00. After watching the famous boxer Mohammad Ali, Stallone came up with an idea for a movie, and began writing a script for it. After three days of minimal sleep and maximum effort, the movie *Rocky* was born, launching Stallone to Hollywood stardom. Everyone can agree that at this point in his life, Sylvester Stallone could have given up, and no one would blame him; he could've stopped caring for acting, let his failures engross him, and never make it to the fame he is known for today. But Stallone did the opposite, and used his failures to understand which direction he needed to go in. As Stallone once said, "Life's not about how hard of a hit you can give…it's about how many you can take, and still keep moving forward."

Steve Jobs, one of the most influential people in the technological world, was fired from Apple in 1985. Less than a year later, after not giving up on his dreams, Jobs began investing in what became Pixar Animation Studios. Within a few years, Jobs owned 100 percent of Pixar, and in 1996, Jobs returned to Apple to become its CEO. Little did Apple know that the man they had fired would return over a decade later and flip the company on its head, from a falling company to the head technological corporation we know today. This success can only be attributed to Steve Jobs' consistent efforts and his steadfast belief in not allowing life's failures to bring you down. "Sometimes life's going to hit you in the head with a brick. Don't lose faith." (Steve Jobs)

Once you learn how to shape your attitude towards failure, you can begin shaping failure from being setback to advantage; you can begin turning the failure into a learning experience. This can be done in one of two ways: you can either focus on a small scale, and look at the task at hand or short-term goal, or you can focus on the large-scale picture, of where you want to end up in life.

Imagine you're living the life of college freshman. You've begun your college career only a few days ago, and, being an inexperienced student, you accidentally enrolled in a class with the hardest professor the college has to offer. Not knowing any better, and being accustomed to receiving A's your whole life, you study minimally for the first exam and fail it miserably. Like the man stuck in traffic, you have several options: you can drop the class, give up, and not attain the credits you so desperately need in order to graduate. You can also get angry, throw a fit, and blame the teacher for your failure, but ultimately the only thing that you would achieve is allowing you to express your anger in the short term. By doing this, you will very likely fall into the same hole by the time your second exam comes around. Your last option, is to examine your study habits and the professor's testing style, and learn what a better route would be to achieve academic success from your experience. You may learn that the professor asks questions on topics explained in detail in the assigned textbook, so next time you can study with the text rather than just your notes. You may also learn that his tests contain a lot of concepts that you need to memorize, so before the next exam you can create flashcards to help you learn them better. If your attitude towards failure is one that will help you learn from your mistakes, then you will succeed in the class and take away valuable lessons you would have never been able to if you would not have failed.

We can apply the same way of thinking to a larger scale; imagine that instead of failing one exam you fail multiple classes and need to consider a career path change. While this situation is on a much larger scale, determining you path after college and potentially for the rest of your life, the same idea and thought process of the previous situation applies here. You can decide to drop your career path, making the past several semesters of hard work into a waste of time, or you can take your failures, and turn them into your motivation- use them to push yourself harder towards achieving your goal. Now that the need for better grades is much more evident, you can learn from your failures that academic success has no room for slacking off. The point of education is to learn, so learning from your mistakes is a learned experience in and of itself. You can allow your past mistakes to guide you to become a more rigorous student, a trait that can not only get you the grades you need, but also put you on the top of the class for post-college studies, where your success is much more important, such as graduate and professional schools.

The key to this chapter, and ultimately to the remainder of this book, is that you must want change. Sure, you can tell yourself that you will accept failures, however in order to move forward you must be willing to change and be more than your human nature dictates you to be. You must recognize that something must be changed; learning from your failures, what we've described in this chapter, is recognizing *what* needs to be changed, but the more difficult part, what we will describe in the following 12 chapters, is learning *how* to change, and becoming the change you need to rise above your human nature. Before anyone can forgive you for your failures and continue forward, you must do so yourself.

With every failure comes a decision of how to react and accept it. By accepting your failures and learning how to use them to your advantage, you begin to change them into the success you wish to achieve. You begin to take failure, a natural occurrence, and turn it into a step towards success, defying the nature of those who tend to give up and let their failures bring them down. Life is rough, and reaching your destination will be difficult, however your attitude and reaction to the ride will make all the difference.

Challenge #1:
Next time you fail at something, stop and think of what you can learn from your failure, and try to apply that to your next attempt at success.

Chapter 2: From Misfortune to Opportunity

The ultimate measure of a man is not where he stands in moments of comfort and convenience, but where he stands at times of challenge and controversy.
~Martin Luther King, Jr.

In January of 2017, I, at the time an undergraduate student at Brooklyn College, stumbled upon a great fellowship application. This program would fly me out to Lesbos Island, Greece, over my summer break, and I would volunteer with Syrian Refugees who had escaped their war-torn country. On top of that, as a pre-medical school student, I would have been able to volunteer in medical clinics there, giving me access to both healthcare experience and an amazing résumé booster. I applied, and after about a month, I received an email letting me know that they were impressed with my application and that out of over a hundred applicants, I was chosen along with a select few to interview with them. The interview went well, I discussed the finest details of the program with them, and from there everything was looking great.

A few weeks later, on March 17, 2017, I received the bad news: although the program was impressed with my application, they had decided to move forward with other applicants. I was devastated; not only was I not in the program, but my chances looked so good once I got the interview that I hadn't bothered looking into back-up summer plans. Now I was internship-less and summer was closer than ever. A few days later, after tirelessly looking for another program, I opted to volunteer with a different program in Argentina, where I would help provide medical aid for underdeveloped communities in the Cordoba area of the country. While this was definitely a life-changing experience, it was nowhere near the experience I could have had in Greece.

While I was in Argentina, on the morning of June 14, 2017, I woke up to the following headline:

Greece Declares Emergency

After Earthquake Hits Lesbos

According to the article, the "strong earthquake struck the island, killing a woman, injuring several people and leaving hundreds of residents homeless." (Kitsantonis, Greece Declares Emergency After Earthquake Hits Lesbos)

You could imagine the shock on my face; if I had gotten into the program as I had expected, I could have been injured, or worse. The fact that I had not been accepted to the program was already surprising enough, but to think that the misfortune which had caused me so much distress would actually end up saving my life was simply unbelievable! And if you think the story is finished, continue reading.

While the internship in Lesbos would have taken up the entirety of my summer, the volunteering program in Argentina lasted only a month. To fill up the remainder of my time, I had decided to take two medical certification night courses back at home, to become a certified phlebotomist and EKG technician. For about a week and a half during that same time period, I had shadowed a cardio-thoracic surgeon at Weill Cornell Medical College on the Upper East Side of Manhattan, making my days and evenings very busy.

On Monday evening, August 14, 2017, I had decided that I was going to ditch class in order to attend a boat party a lot of my friends were attending. The party was a lot of fun, at least until the end. As the boat started heading back towards the dock, and as I was making conversation with somebody I had met, a friend of mine ran up to me and yanked my arm. "Someone's having an asthma attack," I remember her saying vividly. My friend, knowing that I was a certified EMT, thought that I would be the best fit to handle the situation.

I followed her to the center of the dance floor, where I saw the young woman sitting on the floor. She had happened to be an EMT too, and had no difficulty describing how she felt and giving me the information she knew would help me. However, as we were speaking, she fainted. I checked her pulse and breathing, and she still had a pulse but had stopped breathing. In a situation like this, the best form of treating someone is to give the patient rescue breaths, or more commonly known as mouth to mouth. Usually, an EMT would not give mouth to mouth to anybody without a separation device to protect them from potential diseases the patient may carry, however, I decided that, based on the fact that we had several mutual friends and that she came from a very religious community, I would give her mouth to mouth anyways. In my mind, the risk for contracting a disease was outweighed by the danger she faced at that current moment.

I was wrong. After I began doing what I believed was the right thing to do, I heard one of her friends, standing a few feet away from me, say that just last week the girl I was saving had mono, otherwise known as the "kissing disease." I was terrified, however I continued doing what I was doing because I knew that if I had contracted any sickness it would be too late, and I gave her off to the paramedics when they arrived.

I thought of going to my primary care physician to be tested for mono, just in case I had contracted it, however I found myself too busy between shadowing and classes to make time for it. That same week, on Friday morning, I woke up extremely ill; I couldn't eat anything all day, had a pounding headache, and was weak. Fortunately, that happened on a Friday, the one day a week I did not have classes nor shadowing at Weill Cornell. I made an appointment with my doctor for that day.

After recounting my story to the doctor, he checked me for mono and informed me that I was clean from the disease and that my symptoms would pass in a day or two. The doctor curiously asked me about my summer so far and how I had been spending my time. I told him about my certification courses and other experiences that summer, and he was impressed. He was so impressed, that he offered me a position to work for him as a Medical Assistant. Not only was this a paid position, it also gave me much more healthcare experience and was a much better résumé booster than the Greece experience would have ever given me.

The reason for this lengthy story isn't to simply amuse you; I added this story here in order to share the lesson I learned from this summer, which is to not to take misfortune shallowly. Even the worst of misfortune could become the greatest blessing for a person, it's just a matter of how you approach and how you react to it. In other words, misfortune is a game of the mind, not a characteristic of an event.

There are two types of misfortunes in the world: those that are caused by our own actions and those that are exogenous, caused by the world around us. We call misfortunes that are the product of our own actions, failure. Every action we take is an attempt to achieve something for our own benefit, and when that action deviates from benefitting us, we say that we have failed in that action. We have discussed failures and how to use them as a stepping stool for growth in the previous chapter, and in this chapter we will focus on the other type of misfortune: those that are out of your control. While both types of misfortune come from different entities, they both teach us the same life lesson: instead of letting the adversity bring you down, you can use it for your own benefit by changing your attitude towards it.

Besides for the difference in source, there is one other fundamental difference between failures and exogenous misfortunes; failures can for the most part be prevented, misfortunes cannot. As described in the previous chapter, if you fail at a task, you need to learn from the mistake and allow it to guide you on your next attempt at success. However, for exogenous misfortunes, it is impossible to prevent. Life throws curve balls from all directions, and while we learn to swing the bat and hit home-runs, the pitcher of life doesn't run out of baseballs and doesn't stop pitching.

Just because we cannot prevent exogenous events from taking place does not mean we can't learn how to accept and grow from them. Instead of seeing misfortune as a negative event which causes us distress, we can view them as opportunities to grow. While the key to changing failure to success laid in attitude, the key to turning adversity to opportunity lies in reflection.

Reflection is an after-the-fact action that enables us to overcome the stress and anxiety caused by misfortune and turn them into opportunities. Using reflection, we learn to not only not fall, but to persevere and grow. In order to reflect properly on an event, in a way that will guide us towards a proper response, several steps must be taken.

By continuing to read further, you are already beginning to practice the first step of reflection: sitting down and thinking about what had happened. You recognize that post-misfortune contemplation is needed, and that recognition alone can push the entire reflection process towards success. In psychology, there is a term used regarding people who try solving the stress of misfortunes by forgetting and ignoring it; *avoidance*. Avoidance, in essence, is the opposite of reflection. Instead of confronting a misfortune to learn and improve, avoidance simply delays the effort needed to overcome it, and may enhance the suffering misfortune can cause if handled ineffectively.

The second step is recognizing that we have limited knowledge on the effects the misfortune will have on the world's timeline. This may seem cliché, but in reality none of us know what the direct and indirect effects of life events will be, and if we cannot predict the future, how can we really know what events are misfortunes and which are blessings? As the old Yiddish adage goes, "Man Plans, and God laughs." What if the train getting stuck on the way to work prevented us from getting into a car accident if we were to cross the street by the station five minutes earlier? What if becoming sick and needing to stay at home prevented you from making a mistake and getting fired from your job had you had gone to work that day? The truth is, whether we attribute misfortune to a divine power or to natural occurrences, we, with our limited perspective and knowledge of how events will play out, can never really know whether or not life events are in fact good or bad.

In The Apology of Socrates, by the Ancient Greek philosopher Plato, Plato quotes Socrates as saying "I know that I am intelligent because I know that I know nothing." In this account, Socrates was defending his actions during trial, where the Greek authorities of the time were trying him for corrupting the youth with his philosophical teachings and for not believing in the Greek gods. Socrates was found guilty, and when sentenced to death, he publicly claimed that he did not fear the sentence. "No man knows whether death may not even turn out to be the greatest blessing for a human being; and yet people fear it as if they knew for certain that is is the greatest of evil." (Apology) Socrates became aware of the contradiction of fearing or stressing over the unknown; if we have no way of knowing whether something is good or bad, a blessing or a curse, then why let it bring you down? While Socrates specifically spoke of death, unfortunate events occur in the same way- they may seem to be bad, but in reality we have no way of knowing what the future holds as a result.

Now, in no way am I arguing that all suffering should be ignored or misattributed as benefits; I argue quite the contrary. While we must constantly fight against suffering that can be prevented, we must also acknowledge that even if we cannot prevent a misfortune from occurring, we can always control our reaction towards it. This second step of reflection is the best way to reach a successful reaction towards the misfortune. Once we understand that we are limited in our understanding of the world and its timeline, we can begin to worry less about the event itself, and focus more on how we get through it, leading us to the final step of reflection: strategy.

Strategizing is more than just acting upon an instinct- it means carefully planning, analyzing possible options, and deciding what the best course of action to take would be. Once you have recognized that the event has happened and that it wasn't in your control, or more precisely that it wasn't your fault, you can begin to plan out your reaction towards it. First, you must, in your mind or on paper, make a list of all of the possible options you have on how to react to the situation at hand. If your misfortune was caused by a close friend of yours, for example, you can either get mad and scream at them, you can cut them out of your life and not be friends with them anymore, or you can talk about it with them and move on. Strategizing must be done from a logical point of view, without letting emotions take control of your thoughts, a topic we will discuss in a later chapter.

Next, you need to weigh the consequences of each option. In one situation, screaming at your friend may make your relationship tense and uncomfortable, and discussing how the problem was perceived from both sides may be the best way of moving on. In another situation, maybe this misfortune helps you realize that your relationship is toxic and that it's time to cut this friend out of your life and move on to better people. Either way, you end up in a better place than you would have been originally, either by gaining a deeper understanding of your friend and how to improve your relationship, or by pruning your friends group and moving on to people more suited for you. The real challenge is, however, to choose the right option for the right scenario; if you cut a friend from your life, but the issue was relatively minor and you both really care for each other, then you've missed out on an opportunity to build a strong and potentially long lasting friendship. Our reaction to adversity ultimately makes or breaks the potential of the "unfortunate" event, by either letting it get to you and bring you down, or by letting you get to it and bring yourself up; it's up to you to decide which one you will end up with.

Most times, when people stress over a problem, it's because they really have two problems: the first is the actual problem they are facing, and the second is that they don't have a magical, divine, spectacular way of fixing it. The second problem is a con artist- he hides so you don't even notice him at first (that is, you do not realize that not having a way to fix it is causing stress in and of itself), but then when you realize that he exists (after you stress, when you realize that you need a response because stressing is not going to end it), he seems impossible to fix. Where are you going to find a magical answer to your problem? This is where he gets you; this problem seems the hardest to answer, yet the magical, divine, spectacular answer you look for is the problem itself. By not having a magical way of fixing your problems, you force yourself to work, hope, and persevere, and the result itself is unbelievable. The ability we all have to push through hard times and create a better future we can be proud of is in itself magical, divine, and spectacular- it's just up to us to believe it and make it happen.

Challenge #2:

Next time a misfortune occurs in your life that's out of your control, remember that it may not be such a misfortune, only time will tell. Use that mentality to analyze your possible responses before you respond, and make the smart choice before acting.

Chapter 3: The Ultimate Investment

"Kindness is the language which the deaf can hear and the blind can see." ~Mark Twain

Josh loves fish; ever since Josh was young, his mother fed him fish. One day, Josh was eating a nice fish dinner, and a man approached him. "Young man, why are you eating fish?" the man asked. "Because I love fish," Josh replied. The man looked down at his plate, then back at the man. "You're a liar, you don't love fish. If you loved fish, you would not have plucked it from its home in the ocean, killed, and ate it."

The above analogy was told by Rabbi Abraham Twerski. The point of Rabbi Twerski's story was in order to differentiate between true love, one on the basis of giving, and what he calls "fish love," love which is made of selfish intent. He explains that when you eat fish, you do not really love the fish, you simply love the taste of it for yourself, and use the fish as a "vehicle for your gratification."

True love, on the other hand, is derived from fish love; everybody loves themselves, it's human nature. By giving to others you are investing yourself in those around you. This little part of yourself, which you have placed in others, mirrors your own self-concept, and you begin to love that person because you are now a part of them and their lives. Many people believe that you give to those you love, when in reality the ones you give to become those that are loved.

More frequently than not, the exogenous misfortunes we have in life, as described in the last chapter, are caused by those around us. They can be members of our family, friends, coworkers, etc. What makes these misfortunes different from others, however, is that these have a source of blame.

When you have no source to assign blame for your issues, many different feelings can build up inside of you, influencing how you respond to the situation; you feel confused, helpless, sad, and other types of emotions. However, when a misfortune is the direct cause of another human being, one emotion predominates: anger. Since you can place blame on the other person, you manifest that ability as anger towards them for causing the misfortune.

Anger by itself isn't a bad emotion. If we didn't have anger, people would not call the police after being robbed. They would be scared at the moment, but after the fact they would just feel guilty that they did not walk on a different street and sad that they don't have their wallet anymore, but not angry that the other person caused them harm. When alone, anger can even be a beneficial emotion, a problem arises when people act on that anger, what we call *revenge*.

Revenge is an act one takes in order to

compensate for the misdeeds of another. In short, when somebody, person A, causes a misfortune to another, person B, person B will many times want to "repay" the misdeed by causing a misfortune to person A. After this "compensation," person A will want to take the situation a step further, and cause yet another misfortune to person B, because they have overcompensated. In person A's mind, it would only be fair to give the extra compensation back to person B, that way they will be "even." This ultimately results in a cycle of misdeeds going back and forth between both parties. This cycle is called a *feud*, and only ends when one side gives up angrily. Even though person A and person B may stop causing harm to each other, the bitter taste the other left in their mouth will be very hard to overcome.

The reason the words *compensation, repay*, and *even* are in quotation marks is because these words reflect the mental process of a person taking revenge. These mental processes are subjective to that person, and do not reflect reality. Unfortunately, many people make a false connection between *revenge* and *justice*; they believe that taking revenge is a way of bringing justice to their wrongdoings. Revenge, however, is simply a means of expressing their frustration actively. This is an example of, what is called in psychology, a confirmation bias. Confirmation bias is the idea that people will favor facts and observations which confirm existing beliefs rather than deny them. For example, let's imagine somebody is racist against African Americans and believes that all African Americans are criminals. If one day he sees in the news that an African American was arrested for shoplifting, he will use that to support his belief that all African Americans are criminals. On the other hand, if he sees on the news that an African American bystander witnessed a shoplifting event in action and stopped the robber, his beliefs would be shaped less by that new event than when the African American was the criminal himself.

So if not to take revenge, then what's the proper response to somebody who has caused you a misfortune? Well that depends on what the misfortune was, the relationship between you and that person, and whether or not the misfortune was caused intentionally.

If the misfortune was something of no or little significance to you, then the idea of revenge should not even occur to you to begin with. Let's imagine that somebody driving in the car behind you accidentally honked their horn at you; getting out of the car and threatening their life would be a bit out of proportion. If, on the other hand, the person driving behind you was speeding when you were slowly coming to a stop, and ended up slamming into you and destroying your rear bumper, you would probably get out of the car and approach them. Opening your trunk, grabbing a bat, and smashing the driver's windows, however, would be a terrible option to take, even though confrontation is needed here. If you were to smash this driver's windows, he or she would probably get out of their car and swing a fist at you. In this situation, a good option may be to stay calm, even though you're furious, and nicely speak to the other driver. Tell them that accidents happen, it's no big deal, and then work out with him or her the payment for the damage. If you are sweet and gentle to the other driver, it is very likely that they will accommodate your requests rather than if you had approached them threateningly with a bat.

Now imagine the above scenario, however the other driver was your younger brother, a new driver, and he was driving your parents' car. In this situation, you'd probably be more hesitant about smashing the windows of your parents car. Instead, you may be more inclined to scream at him and tell him how all he knows how to do is cause trouble. While that may be tempting, all it would do is cause conflict between you two and family tension. A better option may be again to stay relaxed, and instead of screaming, use a hushed and kind tone to express your disdain at his actions, and tell him that you will discuss with your parents how to avoid future accidents and pay for the reparations later that day at dinner. By being kind and showing love to your brother, you are much more likely to gain his respect and influence him. This way, you can get your care repaired, teach your younger brother a valuable life lesson, and, most importantly, keep your cool and stay happy.

Now, imagine the opposite scenario: the driver who hit you was obviously drunk. You know that his intentions were to drink and drive, making his error not an accident anymore. Instead of shattering his windows, you politely ask him to pull over and park (or park for him so that he doesn't cause more damage), and offer to drive him home before informing the police. If he is hesitant, or you are uncomfortable with driving an intoxicated stranger home, being polite and avoiding conflict while calling the police would save you a lot of trouble, especially since you would be dealing with somebody who has no control over his reaction, including his inclination of taking revenge.

But why does being kind at a time of misfortune work so well? It is simply because you are defying your human instinct. When somebody causes another harm, they expect an angry and vengeful response from the person whom they've hurt. If you approach them and respond with kindness, you are going against their expectations. This defiance confuses your counterpart, forcing them to use their mental energy and carefully plan out their response to your kindness. Given that they are now thinking more carefully about their response, more reasonably rather than emotionally, they are very likely to reciprocate the kindness rather than respond with hostility.

Kindness is a powerful tool in time of conflict, and is even more effective when you are not facing conflict. When you show kindness to people for absolutely no reason, you cause two things: you make the person on the receiving end of the kindness less prone to causing you misfortune, and you slowly alter your personality and mentality to a more lovable one.

For the first, doing random acts of kindness causes people to be less likely to cause you harm. Your kindness will make the other person want to reciprocate it, and they will ultimately be more careful not to cause you harm. Harm can even be the simplest and most insignificant of all things, such as saying the wrong word to somebody. Even if you deserve it they will be more hesitant. For example, if you offer your friend a ride home after work, they would be more likely to not criticize you in front of your boss· the next day. They will be extra careful to be nice to you, because you were nice to them. Because your friend enjoyed the good feeling you gave them when you offered them a ride home, they will act kindly towards you so that they can feel that feeling again in the future.

Not only will the other person be careful not to cause you a misfortune, but they will also feel obligated to you, in a psychological sense. In social psychology, this is called *reciprocity*. Reciprocity is the feeling of obligation a person feels to return positivity to somebody who has done a positive act for them. So again, let's say you offer your friend a ride home from work one evening. Your friend now, even if they are unaware of it, feels obligated to reciprocate the positivity, so they may offer you a helping hand next time they see you could use one.

Note the similarity between the concept of *reciprocity* and *revenge*. They are both really the same, each only differing in the intentions behind them. Revenge is human nature telling you to return negativity with negativity while reciprocity is it saying to return positivity with positivity. These two concepts compete for your mentality. Somebody who is equally inclined to reciprocate positivity with positivity and negativity with negativity is simply human, not exceeding nor falling behind in his human capabilities. However, if you are trying to live your life with a more positive lifestyle, thus exceeding your expectations and rising above human nature, the challenge is to break the negativity of revenge and replace it with positivity. This boosts your inclination of reciprocity and thus boosts your positive outlook on life.

The second effect of showing kindness is that it changes your personality and mentality. As described with the analogy of Josh in the beginning of the chapter, true love is a love of giving without return. When a person gives, they invest themselves in another, and love them as they love themselves. The similarity between the love you feel for the other person and the love you feel towards yourself depends on how much you invest in them. Imagine you are an overall kind and giving person; you give to all people, whether they be friends or strangers, and therefore have a small investment in all of the people around you. You will be known for always being upbeat and spreading joy. This is especially true when your kindness is not meant to reciprocate another's initial kindness. By beginning to show random acts of kindness towards everybody, especially when it is uncalled for, the kindness ceases to be random; it begins to be kindness in order to bolster the well-being of that whom you've invested in, and now love.

Your investment in all people is like owning stocks in every stock in the stock market; the amount of ownership you have in each company differs depending on how much you invest in them ,however you still care for every company's well-being. When you care for everybody's wellbeing, everybody will begin to reciprocate by caring for your well-being, at least to some degree.

Now the questions arise of how can you show kindness to everybody. Imagine offering to drive every single coworker you have a ride home from work; it's an impossible task, at the very least. This is why it's important to define what constitutes as an "act of kindness." For the purposes discussed in this chapter, an "act of kindness" can be as simple as saying a nice word to somebody. For example, saying a kind "thank you," to the bus driver as you exit the bus to get to work is a way of being kind. If you commute at the same time every morning and see the same bus driver often, you will notice after some time that they will begin to be kind to you in return. Their reciprocated kindness may be hard to pick up on, but it would most likely manifest itself as a them responding "You're very welcome" with a kinder tone and a smile on their face, rather than a stern "no problem" they give everybody out of habit.

Even your choice of words can impact how you display kindness to others. Notice how in the previous paragraph the bus driver used the words "you're very welcome," and "no problem," to express the same thing, but to two different people.

It was told to me once by a psychologist at Brooklyn College that the difference between the words "my pleasure," and "no problem," is extraordinary. Even though you may not notice it, the implications of each term is picked up by those we speak to. The words "no problem," imply that the favor done to the other was simply because it was of no hassle to them. This also implies that if doing the favor was "in the way" of their normal routine, they probably wouldn't do it. "My pleasure," on the other hand, implies that not only did one person do you a favor, however helping you also brought them pleasure. In other words, they would be delighted to help you again in the future, even if it gets in their way. A simple change in two words makes the difference between a common helping hand to a kind favor and investment in the other.

The idea behind doing small acts of kindness, even if it is simply giving a kind word to a stranger, is that what costs you nothing may be of infinite value to another. To give you an example of this, the following event happened to me about a week before writing this chapter.

I was sitting at home one day watching TV, and all of a sudden my phone buzzed- it was a text message from my girlfriend. To give some context, the creative writing club at Brooklyn College, Stuck in the Library, was publishing a poetry magazine in which I had submitted a poem several months prior to receiving that text. Little did I know at the time that the new president of the club, Mary, would become my girlfriend just a month or two later. My poem, titled "Jerusalem of Gold," was one of my most proud poems, and the one I had submitted to the magazine.

Now, fast-forward to the day I had received the text from Mary. Mary was on a trip in Israel, and that morning she had arrived with the group she had traveled with to Jerusalem. I opened up the text message to be surprised by the picture you can see on the next page.

I was amazed; not only was Mary thinking of me while having the time of her life on a trip, but she had also remembered the poem I wrote before we even began dating. I don't remember the last time I had seen something so thoughtful and heartfelt.

For Mary, taking a picture of that page probably took no more than 15 seconds of her life, cost her absolutely nothing, yet still meant the world to me. This is the power of kindness: it's free, yet also priceless.

Adapted from the short story, "The Star Thrower," by Loren Eiseley, is an anecdote that illustrates this important concept:

An older man was sitting on the beach as he did every morning, drinking his coffee and reading the morning paper. The night before there had been a storm, and thousands of starfish had washed up on shore. The man looked up from his article, and noticed a young boy standing at the edge of the sea. The boy slowly bent down, picked up a starfish off of the wet sand, and threw it into the waves in front of them.

After watching the boy throw several starfish, the man decided to approach him. "Young boy," the man asked, "why are you throwing the starfish into the ocean?"

"The sun is up and the tide is going out, and if I don't throw them back into the ocean they will surely die!" the boy replied.

"But young man," the older man replied, "There are thousands of starfish along the shore, there is no way you will be able to make a difference."

The young boy bent down, picked up another starfish, and threw it into the ocean. "It made a difference for that one." The old man, astonished by the young boy's wisdom, bent down, picked up a starfish, and threw it into the ocean with.

People around you are starfish, and the world is the beach. Surely you cannot change every starfish you meet, but you can change the world for every starfish.

Challenge #3:

Keep an eye out for your next

opportunity to show kindness to another, or just give over a nice word to them, even if they're a stranger to you. Invest yourself in those around you, and you will find yourself loving everyone more, including yourself.

Chapter 4: The Power of Forgiving

"To forgive is to set a prisoner free and discover that the prisoner was you"
~Lewis B. Smedes

Many scientists argue that the most complex object that exists in the known universe is the human brain. The human brain contains approximately 100 billion neurons, each containing a copy of about 20,000 genes, each coding for a different protein to carry out a different function. Stemming from this object is what we call the mind, what we perceive as consciousness.

If you think about it, everything you know about the world is due to the functioning of your mind; your brain may pick up a signal from one of your senses and interpret it to be a sound, feeling, or vision, however it is your higher functioning capabilities, your deeper understanding of the sense, which ultimately decides the fate of your experience. Your memories, decisions, experiences, and everything else that makes you you, and not a robot, comes from your mind.

While we all have this complex mind contained in us, we get used to the fact that we are human; as we grow, we become accustomed to the world we live in, and we take for granted how complex and intricate the world really is. The only thing each individual truly understands is their own mind. Not everybody is a neuroscientist, and not everybody knows the basics to how the brain works, however everybody does know their own cognitive processes and how they think about the world.

Since it's hard for most people to imagine a world of eight billion minds of equal complexities to their own, people usually dismiss this notion by believing they are superior to everyone around them. Put simply, everybody thinks that they know better than the people they interact with. When somebody who practices this while being aware of it, and consciously believes that they are superior, they are a narcissist. This person becomes overjoyed from their own mental capabilities, and fails to recognize the value of the minds surrounding him because he is too obsessed with his own. In the narcissist's mind, his superiority means that he is his best investment, and if he is his best investment, he should not and will not invest in others by showing them kindness. Extrapolating from what we described before, one who cannot invest in others and be kind to those around him is unable to love. You will also rarely find a narcissist who will admit to their own narcissism. The narcissist is oblivious to his own narcissism because he refuses to accept the complexity of everybody else's mind, and he then begins to deny his own self-absorbed manner.

Once we allow ourselves to accept that every human in the world has a mind as complex as our own, we can begin to see the actions of others in a clearer way, from a different perspective. When a person makes an error, we tend to get angry at them (depending on the magnitude of their error, of course), a natural human instinct. While in Chapter 2 we dealt with *how* to manage your response to misfortunes caused by the world around you, including other people in your life, in this chapter we will deal with *when* it is proper to respond, and when it is proper to forgive.

Surely you have been asked in the past what you would do in a situation "if you were in another's shoes." This question is not void of a deeper meaning. Many times we judge people's actions using a third person perspective. However, if we can imagine ourselves in the same situation as those we are judging, our opinion of how they have acted may change. When we equate a person's actions with themselves, a different person, we judge their actions from a third person perspective. This third person perspective is one that looks down at others as inferior and us as superior, and that leads to narcissism. Instead, if we equate others and their actions to ourselves, we begin to judge their actions from a first person perspective, by wearing their shoes. This is a common psychological phenomenon, termed the foundational attributional error. In this phenomenon, a person is likely to attribute their own wrongdoings as consequences of circumstances out of their control (giving themselves excuses), and blaming people's inner thinking and personality when they cause a misfortune. We will return to this concept in future chapters, because it is important to understand that our own perspective is biased when compared to the objective truth of a situation. When we begin to see from the perspective of those that are mistaking, we can understand the inner mechanics of their minds and thought processes, and come to less angry conclusions- those of forgiveness.

Forgiveness is the greatest kindness one can do for another. Any other kindness is directed towards a person whom you care about, and are happy with, or towards a stranger, who you are neutral towards. Forgiveness, on the other hand, is an act of good will and investment made in those who have faulted you, those whom you have negative feelings towards. While we may love and care deeply for those we forgive, they have still faulted us in some way or another, making it much harder to show kindness and love towards them.

While forgiveness is a much harder act of kindness to achieve, the rewards of forgiving are much greater too. By forgiving somebody for a wrongdoing, you not only invest in them, rather you also show them that you are investing in them; in this situation, the other becomes aware of your investment rather than it just occurring naturally. Most kindnesses do not openly express your investment and care for the other, however when you show the kindness of forgiving to someone when you have a very clear reason to be upset with them, even temporarily, you are telling them that you care for your relationship and your future with them. As with other kindnesses, the one being forgiven will be inclined to reciprocate love and kindness towards you, especially if you wrong them one day, however their knowledge of your kindness will make the drive to reciprocate even stronger.

As Martin Luther King Jr. once said, "He who is devoid of the power to forgive is devoid of the power to love." We all have the power to be kind and learn to love others, however the power of forgiveness is crucial to being able to fully love. Using the analogy of stocks again, without forgiveness you are an uneducated stock owner tossing money around in the air; you show kindness to everybody, but if you cannot forgive an investment when they wrong you, you are bound to lose all of the love you have worked hard to earn.

The ideology of the narcissist can be used to bolster forgiveness rather than fight it, depending on how you use it. To reiterate the narcissist's ideology, the narcissist believes that he is superior, and therefore he is his own best investment. It is his human nature making him believe that he is on top, however it is his weakness in manipulating that inclination that gives him the title of a narcissist. On the other hand, a person who knows how to manipulate his natural instinct to be on top will reason in the following way: by not forgiving someone who has wronged you, you leave them in their position of weakness, and find superiority in that you are in a higher position, psychologically, than they are (because they have faulted and you have not, therefore you are superior to them). Even if the other person does not think they have faulted, you believe they have, and therefore in your mind they are at a low position, one of of weakness and vulnerability to criticism. Keep in mind that these terms of superiority and inferiority are relative to your own self evaluation or how you feel about yourself, your self-esteem. While you feel in power because you are higher than they are, in reality you have not risen to any higher level than you were before the incident took place. Your counterpart has acted wrongly, thus lowering how you feel about them, rather you remain in the same spot. If you learn to forgive, you begin to see your position of power in a different way; by forgiving the other person, you are telling them that they have fallen, but that you will allow them to rise again and learn from their mistakes. This makes the person at fault rise back up towards their original position, even if only partially. In your mind, two thing occur as a result of this: you feel empowered by being able to rise above your human nature and forgive, what we mean when we tell people to "be the bigger man," and you also feel superior in that the person at fault only rose back due to your action. In your mind you have both helped the other person rise, and have risen yourself too. And to make yourself feel even better, forgiving has saved you a lot of unnecessary negative emotions which you would have held on to had you not have forgave.

When you forgive, you invest in others and ultimately in yourself in the long term. In contrast, remaining angry and clinging onto misfortunes only makes you feel good, or superior, temporarily. Your anger will fade over time naturally, even if you've never forgiven the other person and you hold onto anger for a long time, and you miss out on an opportunity to grow in personality and live a happier lifestyle. A mistake is a pencil mark and can be erased, but forgiveness is written in permanent marker on another's heart.

Challenge #4:

If you encounter a situation where somebody has wronged you, take a moment to think logically, do not let emotions cloud your vision, and imagine how you would act if you were in the other person's position. Learn to understand people from their perspective, and forgive their errors because they will grow, you will grow, and you'll both be happier.

Chapter 5: The Leader in You

"Be the change you wish to see in the world" ~Mahatma Gandhi

"Be a leader." How many times have you heard people say that to you? From the moment you understood what leadership was, every person around you tried convincing you to be a leader. But what makes somebody a leader? What defines leadership? Does being in a position of power make you a leader? Many times, the answers to all of these questions go unanswered. This is because most people simply don't understand the questions themselves to begin with; they take the word *leadership* for granted, without giving thought to its true meaning.

The first thing to do in defining leadership, and ultimately becoming a leader, is to examine different leaders throughout history and find similarities in their character traits. Note how similarities in their character traits was specified rather than their actions; this is because what makes a person a leader are the traits they have internalized rather than external forces giving them power.

Before examining different leaders' character traits, let's give a general definition of a leader, one which we will refine over the next few chapters, as an origin for our discussion. A leader, in the general sense, is a person who has influence over a group of people. In common language, we would call anybody who has any sort of influence over others a leader, however for our purposes we will define a leader as somebody who has influence over the way people think. This is because somebody may be able to impose requirements over others using their position of power, however those whom the new required acts are being imposed on rarely ever agree with them; they generally act out of fear of punishment. A good example of this would be a government official raising the tax requirements over a population of people. Nobody likes paying the extra taxes, however everyone agrees to do so out of fear of punishment. The punishment of not paying the additional tax far outweighs the annoyance of the extra fee. Somebody who is able to inspire or motivate the masses, on the other hand, can and will influence the way people think. By shifting the way people think, people will begin to act accordingly. This ultimately achieves the same goal as the government official, however here the leader is creating a more unified population acting for a common goal.

Every third grade student can tell you that Abraham Lincoln was the president of the United States of America, but what made Abraham Lincoln a leader? Well, one of Lincoln's most famous quotes is "A house divided against itself cannot stand." Lincoln was talking about the divided nation fighting against each other during the Civil War, however he had a deeper understanding of leadership. Abraham Lincoln understood that being a leader involves keeping the mass undivided. A unity is an entity of the mind, and an entity of the mind can only be formed through influence of the mind rather than being forced upon the body and its possessions.

Another influential figure in history was Winston Churchill. Churchill was the British Prime Minister during World War II, and is most famous for not only leading Great Britain to victory with the Allied Powers, but also for inspiring the nation to keep strong during the difficult war. During World War II, Churchill famously said the following: "We shall defend our island, whatever the cost may be, we shall fight on the beaches, we shall fight on the landing grounds, we shall fight in the fields and in the streets, we shall fight in the hills; we shall never surrender." There are two words that deserve special attention here: the word *we* and the word *shall.*

When Churchill used the word "we," he was doing something similar to what Lincoln was doing-Churchill was uniting his nation. He was creating a sense of *belonging.* In psychology, belongingness is a feeling of being part of a group. When one has a sense of belonging, the group they are a part of becomes a part of their identity. By making his audience feel like they were part of a collective group, Churchill made each individual believe that they belonged to a purpose that was bigger than themselves. Once a person feels that they are part of a larger purpose, their decision making is influenced also by the goals of the collective rather than only their individual motives.

In order to influence the way people think, you must understand the mechanics of their minds and look at the world from their perspective, similar to how you would when forgiving. Take a second, and think about how you view the world. Think about who you care the most about, what your daily life looks like, what you value most in yourself and in others, etc. The way a person observes the world, and everything that goes on in it, is the glasses they wear when they step foot outside. Everything a person experiences is modified and effected by these glasses, thus effecting their *perception* of the world. In neuroscience, perception is defined in contrast to sensation. Sensation is the physical reception of a stimulus, such as your eyes picking up light, your nose picking up a scent, etc. Perception, on the other hand, is the understanding of the sensation; turning the light into a beautiful painting, or the scent into perfume. Every person has their individual prescription, and you can have an influence over them, without ever changing the person's physical body, by changing their prescription.

The tool that is most effective at changing one's perception of reality are words. While words can be an incredible tool for influencing other's perception of the world, the real skill lies in how you use them. A person who uses his words as a tool to inspire and lead, such as Churchill, can build amazing structures. On the other hand, a person who uses the same tools impulsively, can make a fool of himself in the eyes of those around him.

Adolf Hitler, as evil as he was, was extremely skillful at using his words. However, Hitler used his ability to manipulate the German population and perpetrate one of the greatest atrocities in history, the Holocaust. By no means should anybody be praising Hitler and his abilities to make people believe that good is bad and bad is good, rather we should take the misfortune of Hitler's existence and use it to grow, as discussed in Chapter Two. Hitler understood the influential powers of his words, and therefore gave much attention to the words he used when speaking to large audiences. "By the skillful and sustained use of propaganda," Hitler once said, "One can make a people see even heaven as hell or an extremely wretched life as paradise."

Another quote that Hitler is famous for saying is "Words build bridges into unexplored regions." This unexplored region is the mind and perception of those around you. Others' perceptions are "unexplored," because no person can ever really stand in someone else's shoes, as the idiom goes. What a person can do, however, is make another person's eyeglass prescription come close to their own. Once the other person begins wearing glasses very similar to that of your own, you can imagine how it would be to see the world like they do, because you are both seeing the world in very similar ways.

The tool of words is like using a screwdriver to build a structure made of wood; if you turn the screw too little, the structure will be loose and shaky, and if you turn it too much, you can crack the wood in half. You also need to choose the right sized screwdriver before using it, or else you will not accomplish anything. So, how do you choose the right screwdriver and how do you know how much to turn it? The answer lies in the screw itself.

Before speaking, especially if you are trying to persuade somebody to do something, you must analyze their character traits. This is true for strangers, and even more so for people you are close with. By knowing what kind of character a person has, you can determine what they would like to hear. In other words, the more you understand which words will successfully influence somebody, the more successful you will be in using them.

This skill is the difference between speaking in order to speak and speaking in order to be heard. Somebody that speaks just for the sake of speaking can go on for hours without even the slightest consideration for the person they are engaged in conversation with. Somebody who speaks in order to be heard, however, will say what he wants his counterpart to understand. The person who wants to be heard will choose a screwdriver based on the size of the screw rather than the one that fits their hand best. The importance of this is usually felt when engaging in an interview, whether you are the interviewer or the interviewee. If you are trying to inspire somebody to rise up from a bad situation, you may opt to use words of hope rather than pessimism. If you want to give somebody a piece of advice you may choose not to criticize them for their wrongdoings, rather you may touch upon a better route to success that they haven't considered. This also works when speaking to crowds, however when speaking to groups of people, you must consider the wants and needs of the collective rather than the individual when choosing your words wisely.

While understanding the person you are speaking to is paramount to using your words successfully, certain rules exist which apply to almost everybody. Hundreds of books have been written solely on these rules, however we will discuss only three of them here.

First, using a person's name in a sentence is like adding a little spice to a bland meal. The food may still look and smell the same as it had before, however now it is much more flavorful. When you call a person by their name, you make whatever you are saying personal to them, thus making it more "real" in that person's eyes. I say real, because it makes your words a part of their perceived reality. If you were to say the same thing but without using the person's name, your words simply become *your* words and *your* opinion rather than a contribution to *their* reality.

For example, simply saying "thank you" to somebody versus saying "thank you" followed by their name can make a major difference in the perceived gratitude in your words. For the first one, the person receiving the thank you simply receives it as a response to a good deed. The second response, however, is taken as a genuine appreciation of the good deed done. This is because when you used the person's name, you subconsciously activate the recognition that the person themselves did something for you that stands out from others, and they feel special. Another example would be getting an autograph from the celebrity you most admire. If the celebrity addresses your name in the little note they write for you, it is appreciated much more because it is addressed specially and personally to you. the key similarity in these two is that saying a person's name makes them feel like they stand out from the rest, that they are unique and special.

Asking a person about their lives is another great way to gain a person's full interest in a conversation, and thus influence them. I'm sure you can remember a time where you had had conversation with somebody who had only spoke about themselves; it was probably disastrous for you, but heaven for them. When you ask somebody to talk about themselves, you are showing genuine interest in their lives and making the conversation more pleasurable for them. This taps into the other person's human nature to love themselves, and they would be delighted to praise themselves in order to impress you, no matter your relationship to them. Naturally, people care about themselves and their own accomplishments over those of others, even their close family members. Once that person sees that you are interested in what they have to say about themselves, they will naturally be interested in what you have to say because they have already judged the conversation as favorable. This is the same principle we've discussed in Chapter 3, reciprocity. Now that you've gained the other person's interest and attention in what you have to say, you can have influence over their perception of the world.

Lastly, you can do the opposite of the second general rule of influencing others, and do the impressing for them. Giving a person genuine praise rarely fails in persuading them to see the world as you do. When you praise a person, you are showing them that you see potential in them over the average person. For example, if you are trying to persuade your teenage son to put in more effort in his studies, you are more likely to convince him to listen to you if you tell him that he should study because he's smart and has potential for great academic success rather than only stressing that good grades will help him get into a good college in the future. Doing this makes the other person see you as a reliable and caring person, because if you did not care about them you would not put in effort to genuinely praise them. I say genuine intentionally, and that is because people are not as vulnerable to this trick as they may be to the last two. Most people have the ability to read right through ingenuity, especially when you are praising them for something they don't deserve praise for.

If you overdo what you say, and turn the screwdriver too much, you can destroy the entire structure you were working on. This applies to not only the three rules discussed above, but to every strategy you use when trying to influence another person. Speaking strategically is a tool used on the subconscious of the person you are speaking to, and overdoing your effort will bring the tool to their consciousness, their awareness. The same way armies will not use strategies that their enemies are aware of, once the person you are speaking to becomes aware of your efforts and strategies to influence them, you have lost the game. When somebody is aware of another trying to influence them of a certain point, they become more adamant to change. They see another trying to influence them as an infringement on their individuality and right to formulate their own opinions, even if you are trying to influence them on a topic that they previously had no opinion of. This is why it is of extreme importance to not overdo your tactics, and to know when to back down from trying to influence. If you need to back down, you can at least wait for a better opportunity to try again, however if you overdo your efforts you have lost any ability to try again, at least for the near future or on the topic you were trying to influence on.

A person who is adept at using their words to influence those on the receptive end of them can have inconceivable power over their actions and motives, whether for the good or for the bad, to inspire or to manipulate. The question now, however, is how do you learn to use your words for the good rather than the bad?

To extend this question back to the original topic of this chapter, how do you use your ability to influence others in order to become a leader? The answer to this lies in what we call compassion, or empathy. Empathy is the mirroring of emotions and feelings, specifically those of suffering, from one person to another. When somebody observes another person experiencing pain, for example, human nature is to flinch in response to their pain. This is carried out by special neurons in the brain called mirror neurons. These neurons react to stimuli which other people experience, such as pain, and react the same way to the observation as your brain would if you were experiencing such pain. Of course this does not mean that if you were to witness someone get hit by a truck that you would feel their pain identical to the way they do, however you would definitely flinch and feel a quick wave of shock from their pain. This is why if you show people a video of somebody doing something painful, their response is of uncomfort, and sometimes to even say "Ouch."

What makes a person a leader is not that they have only influential skills over the people they are leading, but that this power comes from the heart. As discussed in Chapter 3, when you love somebody it is because you have invested in them and wish only for their best. The same goes for leading; a leader invests himself in his people, and thus wants only the best for them. When they suffer, he suffers, and when they rejoice, he rejoices. This is what drives a leader to continue leading and push for progress, because success of the collective is success for him on a personal level.

A person can be adept at using his words and

empathetic towards his people, however if he never uses those skills he will never be able to lead. So how does one use the skills needed to become a leader? The answer lies in one word: initiative. A leader does the opposite of what's expected; a leader rises up to the challenge and takes the first step towards progress.

When the average person sees an issue that is bigger than themselves, they are inclined to stay idle and wait for somebody else to take action. Although it is in everybody's human nature to alleviate suffering from others, due to empathy, people still tend to ignore situations which don't directly effect them, especially if the way to help is outside of their comfort zone. This is what psychologists call the *bystander effect*. The bystander effect is the human inclination to assume that somebody else will take action in an uncomfortable situation, and therefor you do not need to act directly. This is why, as has been proven time and time again, many people can watch terrible crimes, including rape, murder, and robbery, and not a single person will take action to prevent it. Everybody assumes that somebody else will act, and then nobody acts. This is why most organizations that provide CPR training will teach that the first step you do in an emergency medical situation is to assign the job to call emergency medical services to one specific person. They teach that in order for the ambulance to actually be called, you must point and delegate people. If an emergency were to occur and you were to just yell out "Somebody call an ambulance!" it is likely that nobody will call.

A true leader is the person who will pick up the phone and call the ambulance, the person who will take a hold of his empathy and use that to overcome the bystander effect. Taking initiative is the ultimate cause of having no excuses. When you live life giving yourself no excuses for slacking off, you learn to be responsible. You are responsible for your actions, especially of not acting, and thus you live to make the most of yourself and of everything that comes your way. Why do you think many employers ask on their job applications whether or not an applicant is willing to take initiative? It is for the sole reason that taking initiative shows leadership, responsibility, and a drive for success, all of which employers look for in a potential job candidate.

While in other chapters we have focused on rising above human instincts that have negative impacts on our lives, this chapter focuses on seizing instincts that we already have and using them to their greatest potential. By using your human nature of speech and empathy in the right way, you can rise above your natural tendency to be average and you can make yourself a leader. You are your own change, and you are the leader that will be an example for the world.

Challenge #5:
Make yourself stand out; be smart when you speak, stand up to the challenge next time

you see a problem, and lead. Change in yourself is the mark of leadership.

Chapter 6: The Optimal Emotional Experience

"Holding on to anger is like grasping a hot coal with the intent of throwing it at someone else; you are the one who gets burned." ~Buddha

Have you ever met somebody who was always grouchy? Somebody always on edge, enough that everyone knows that if you get on this person's nerves, even just a little bit, that he would burst into rampage and anger? Once upon a time there was a boy that behaved exactly like that, and his name Billy.

When Billy was seven years old, his parents noticed that he had a very bad temper; every time somebody would ask him to help with something, correct him for behaving a certain way, or even push his buttons just a tiny bit, he would begin to scream and curse at them until they would walk away. They had realized that if they don't act now, Billy would have problems living in society in the future.

Billy's father approached him one day, and told him that there's a new rule in the house: whenever Billy would get angry, he would have to go outside and hammer a nail into their fence. Seeing nothing in this task, Billy complied. After several weeks of this, the fence was covered in nails more than not, and Billy was getting upset with the task getting in the way of his life. He realized that it would be much easier to control his anger than to be hammering nails all day. Gradually, Billy's father had noticed the amount of nails being nailed into the fence decrease.

One evening, Billy had told his father the good news: he had not needed to nail a single nail into the fence that day. His father told him that they're going to change the rule, and that every day he doesn't get angry, he can go to the fence and pull a nail out. After about a year, Billy had reached the final nail in the wall.

"Look at the fence, son, and tell me what you see," Billy's father said. After a long glance at the fence, Billy said "it's full of holes, Papa."

"Yes, son," Billy's father replied, "When you get angry at other people and lose your temper, it's as if you are hammering a nail into their hearts. Even if you apologize and pull the nail out, you have still left a permanent scar on them that cannot bring them back to their original selves."

As we had described in the last chapter, words have tremendous influential power which can be used to build a person into a leader. However, while words have influencing powers over others, there's one thing in this world that has influential powers over words: emotions. When a person is emotionally aroused and allows their emotions to take control of them, they can easily come to say things that they'll regret when they are back in control of themselves. This is because emotions make a person act impulsively rather than rationally; they act and say the first thing that their human nature deems adequate, and skip rationalizing whether or not what they are about to do is appropriate.

Everybody knows what it's like to get angry and temporarily lose control of what you say. Somebody says or does something that upsets you, blood rushes to your face, you ball your fists, and boom- you're angry. This anger may lead to you throwing a punch, saying something inappropriate, etc. In short, you do the first thing that your human instinct tells you to do.

When negative emotions, more so than positive emotions, are involved in a situation, they lead to what is called the *fight or flight* response. This is your body's tendency to either fight and defend itself or run away and avoid a dangerous situation. As humans have evolved, however, our minds began to interpret situations which make us emotionally uncomfortable as dangerous as well, which arose to a fight or flight response in those situations, regardless of their threat to our survival. Imagine yourself in the following situation: somebody walks up to you at night on a dark street, and points a gun at you. What would your natural response be? Most likely you would do one of two things: you'd either run away, or throw a punch at your assailant. Psychologists and neuroscientists have determined a third response, the *freeze* response, where one would just freeze and not react, however we will leave that response on the side.

The fight or flight response is our natural response to stressful situations, therefore making it impulsively driven, or without rational. An impulsive response is one that involves pure human instinct and no rationalizing, and generally leads to unwanted consequences. This is why it is quintessential to learn how to manage your emotions, especially when they have the potential to evoke a fight or flight response.

The best way of managing your emotions is by strengthening what neuroscientists call *metacognition*. Metacognition is the ability to think about thinking itself; to think about one's own thought processes and ability to think. This skill is argued by some to be the fundamental difference between humans from animals. Now, the question is, how can a person strengthen their metacognition? Like anything else, it can be strengthened by constant practice. Metacognition can be easily practiced by actively observing your life from a third person perspective. In any situation, whether negative or positive, imagine yourself floating above the scene and watch how you respond to a situation.

By using this this technique, you can come close to seeing your actions as other people do. When you think about your own actions, you have a personal bias to judge them in a positive light versus when you think about other's actions. In social psychology, this is called the *actor-observer bias*. In this bias, as we had touched upon before, one blames their own actions on external causes when the results are negative and take responsibility for their actions when the results are positive. This avoids the negative feeling associated with negative results of your own actions (what people would call failure, however we've already discussed how to overcome these negative feelings in the first chapter of this book) and promotes the positive feelings associated with success. This is why it is so easy to criticize others when they act inappropriately and point at their bad character traits while it is extremely difficult to do the same towards our own actions. When we begin observing our actions from a third person perspective, we can surpass the actor-observer bias by becoming the observer. Once we become the observer, we can begin to see the traits that are getting in the way of us acting appropriately rather than blaming external causes for the negative results of our actions.

Emotions help us differentiate harm from pleasure, however this differentiation is done very superficially; it is only a short-term differentiation. Emotions help our brains decide how to act quickly in order for us to respond appropriately to a stressful situation without taking too much time. The problem with this, however, is similar to anything else which is done too quickly. As the old adage, adapted from Aesop's fable of the tortoise and the hare, goes, "slow and steady wins the race." When you rush to finish a project, you sacrifice its quality. Yes, its quality can still be close to perfect even when rushed, however the risk of decreasing its quality is much higher when rushed to completion. The same goes for deciding how to respond to a situation; if you take your time and think about your response, you are more likely to respond appropriately. On the other hand, using emotions and acting impulsively, while sometimes giving you accurate and appropriate responses, is more likely to lead you to inappropriate decisions on how to respond. In order to live life to your full potential and rise above your human nature, it is critical that you learn how to take control of your emotions and not the other way around.

As Psychology professor Lisa Feldman-Barrett explains, emotions are "guesses that your brain constructs in the moment...and you have more control over those guesses than you might imagine that you do." Feldman-Barrett explains that people experience the world by predictions. Our brains predict the outcome of an observation based on previous life experiences, such as understanding that a person's facial expressions symbolize anger or joy, excitement or sadness. All this means is that when we see an action or expression being done by others, our perception of it really comes in part from our own minds, and isn't solely based on what they've done, like the glasses each person wears when perceiving the world. Sure, the person is the one doing the action or making the facial expression, but it is our glasses that are making meaning out of it. On top of this, Feldman-Barrett also explains that a person's own emotions work the same way. Our brains assign meaning to different body sensations and predict what they mean, thus creating an emotional response. To use the example that she gave, a churning stomach can occur when walking into a bakery and smelling freshly baked cookies, or it can occur when sitting in a hospital lobby awaiting medical test results. In both scenarios your body has the sensation of a churning stomach, however in one it assigns a feeling of hunger and comfort, and in the other it assigns dread and fear.

Once we understand that our perception of world events comes in part from ourselves, we can partially undo the actor-observer bias. This time, however, we would be undoing it in the opposite way than before. Previously, we undid the bias by becoming the observer of our own actions, whereas this time we become the actors of others' actions. This is because once a person knows that they perceive others' actions through their own perspective, they are less likely to assign blame to them because of their "bad" character traits, because that would be blaming himself in part. Understanding other people's expressions and actions as a part of our own minds' constructs will make pushing blame on them, and thus reacting emotionally and impulsively, a less likely outcome. If you keep this point in mind when you analyze a situation, you can become the master of your brain's predictions rather than the other way around.

True, it isn't as simple as it sounds to change the way your mind makes guesses about the situations around you, however, as Lisa Feldman-

Barrett explains, if you change your perception of a situation today, you are incorporating that perception into your past experiences. Those past experiences are what your brain draws from when making its next prediction, and thus effects your perception tomorrow. So yes, keeping the above point in mind may not instantly help you take hold of your emotional experience, however by practicing it over and over, you add more and more experiences to the tool box your brain will use next time it needs to make a guess on how to react. You will slowly become an expert at controlling those emotional responses, or what Feldman-Barrett calls "an architect of your experience."

One important question to ask is not only *when* to react emotionally, but also *how* to use your emotions when reacting. If you're asked a provocative question, you can't just stand silently and not respond to the person asking the question. True, it would be a bad idea to lash out angrily at them, however surely you will respond to them in one way or another.

With every emotion comes a set of body sensations that are associated with it. It is argued throughout neuroscience whether or not emotions are derived from these sensations or vice versa (whether we interpret body sensations to create emotions or create body sensations based on our emotional experience). Whichever order the emotions and sensations occur, however, we can still take control of them.

If we decide to take the route of emotions preceding the body sensations, then we can control our emotions as described before. If, however, we decide that sensations precede emotions, and that emotions are interpretations of those sensations, we can take control of our emotions by actively taking control of how we interpret those sensations. This is the approach Lisa Feldman-Barrett takes with emotions; if your feel your stomach churn in a hospital awaiting results, you can attribute that feeling to hunger rather than dread. Our minds give meaning to the sensations our body produces naturally, and this is usually done automatically. If we take control of these interpretations, however, we can assign meaning to our body's natural sensations and avoid attributing them to unwanted emotions.

Now imagine you're the manager of a company, and one of the employees made a mistake that could cost the company hundreds of thousands of dollars. Your mind becomes flushed with judgmental thoughts, you feel inclined to take action to destroy the cause of the problems (the "fight" response), and can only think about one thing: ending the situation in a way that puts you on top. Just because you already began feeling angry doesn't mean you can't control your emotional response.

When human nature causes these sensations, people feel impulsive and break out in screaming, anger, and sometimes even violent fits. This is the body trying to protect itself from harm, however it is causing harm to the person themselves. There are other ways these sensations can be used and interpreted, however. Instead of becoming judgmental and judging the employees value and character, the manager can use this increased judgmental awareness to judge the situation and give more attention to different potential pathways the company can take to solve the issue, along with each pathway's consequences (this is an example of strategizing, as we had discussed with dealing with exogenous misfortunes, in Chapter 2). The manager can use his impulse to act as motivation to solve the issue. Yes, the best pathway may be to fire the employee, however it also may not be. Even if it is the correct thing to do, firing the employee harshly and angrily by embarrassing them in front of their coworkers may reflect badly on the company and its values.

Finally, the narrow focus of the manager to end the stress caused by the employee's mistake can be described in one word: determination. Determination is focusing on a goal and making sure you achieve it. If you are determined with focus on your long-term, less impulsive goals (getting the company back to success), that same determination that anger would've used to attack the employee (firing them harshly and bitterly) can be used to solve problems in a very efficient and goal-oriented manner.

The difference between a person who can take control of their emotions and one who cannot is like that of two rafts flowing down a river. One of the rafts contains a person actively rowing and directing his vessel, and the other contains a person flowing naturally with the current. The person in the first raft is in sync with his raft, as they are both harmoniously work with each other in order to direct themselves and reach their destination efficiently. The second person, however, is enslaved to his raft and will end up wherever the raft decides to flow, naturally with the direction of the current. A person who has control of the direction of his emotional experience will feel in harmony with his life and the world around him, whereas one who is enslaved to his human nature will end up wherever it leads him, which most of the times will not be the same as his goals.

Challenge #6:

Take control of your emotions- become aware of how you feel and think in every situation you encounter. Whenever you feel inclined to act out of emotions, or feel body sensations associated with an emotion, try to view them from a third person perspective and judge them and associate the sensations with physical causes. Use your emotions to your advantage, and become the leader of your emotional experience.

Chapter 7: The Judge's Judgment

"When you judge another, you do not define them, you define yourself" ~Wayne Dyer

Judgment: labelling something as good or bad, appropriate or inappropriate, just or unjust, etc. When you judge something, you are rating it in comparison to what you judge as "normal," and normality, as casually as we toss the word around, is not a simple term at all. Normality is a combination of both personal subjectivity and societal objectivity; what each person calls normal is both based on their own personal experiences, and what society tells them normal is.

Personal experience is involved in judgment through a process called *categorization*. The way our brains make sense of the world is by placing every new object we come in contact with into an already existing "category." For example, if you walk into a dining room and see a rectangular piece of wood being held up by pegs, and there are chairs around the structure, you would know that such an object is a table. Even though you've never seen that specific object before, you can still identify it as a table. This is because when you were really young, you were taught that the object in the dining room, the one you sat near in school, the one near your bed, were all "tables." Over time, you have assigned different characteristics to what a "table" is; it has pegs holding it up, we place things on it, there are usually chairs surrounding it, etc. This table that you now have in your brain is an abstract understanding of tables, and is a result of recognizing a pattern of characteristics in objects called "table." This abstract knowledge is a category box, and is used to recognize and identify new tables you encounter throughout your entire life.

The same concept applies to people as well. Through personal experience, your brain recognizes patterns of the people around you: they have two eyes, a mouth, and a nose, all of which lie on their face at a specific size ratio and orientation. People they act a certain way, move in a certain fashion, etc. When you encounter a person that lacks a characteristic you've placed in the "person" category, they are perceived as abnormal. Your brain gets confused as to where it is supposed to place them, and places them in the abnormal box, the box of the unknown. Ultimately, when something fits into a category it is considered "normal," and something that has trouble being placed in a category is thought of as "abnormal."

The second way normality is formed in our brains is through society and social constructs. As we grow from childhood to adulthood, we are taught by society what is accepted and what is not. This is because each society is a big "in-group," an exclusive group of people that share a common characteristic. This common feature can be religious, ethnical, geographical, a shared status (student, employee, etc.), and so on. In-group mentality is studied heavily in Social Psychology, especially in reference to how individuals act in respect to the group they are a part of. A group can have great influence on an individual's decisions and perceptions, and, in contrast, those outside of one's in-group have less of an influence. Those outsiders are called the "out-group," and are seen as different from the members of the in-group. As a person grows, what they define as normal is heavily based on what their society tells them normal is, who can be a part of their in-group, and what abnormal is, who belongs in the out-group.

What's important about the two ways people gain a concept of normality is that either way, what makes the object or person abnormal is not the object or person themselves. In reality, each person's warehouse of categories differ, so it makes sense that one object cannot fit into the same box of every individual. The reason that somebody is perceived as abnormal is not because of their own character traits, rather it is because of the categorization of the one labeling them as abnormal. In simpler terms, the problem with somebody "abnormal" isn't themselves, it's you. If you remember the analogy of perception as glasses, labelling abnormality would be similar placing a small sticker on one of your lenses; just because your glasses do not allow you to see that small area in your vision, does not mean that that spot is not a part of the picture before you.

Previously, I has used the word "problem,"

however abnormality isn't a problem, not for the "abnormal" person nor for you, unless it is acted upon. Abnormality is human nature's self-defense mechanism against the unknown. The unknown, in terms of human nature, always has a potential for danger. This is because when human nature takes over a person, their sole concern is survival. When a person's mind is in survival mode, anything that is not known and recognized is a potential danger. Calling something abnormal only becomes problematic when it is used to cause harm or explain unjust actions, when your human nature tries to eliminate the "danger."

Up until now, all this chapter has done is define how people understand normality and why that understanding is flawed, however it did not add anything new to how we can overcome that humanly way of thinking. We have all been told time and time again that if something seems weird to us, it's us that are at fault and not the thing that is "weird." The question remains, however, how does one stop judging and begin accepting? If categorization is wired into our brains and is the way we make meaning of the world around us, how do we undo the wiring and reconnect the circuits?

Human nature constitutes of being masters of our surroundings. This means that we want to have control and understanding of events that happen around us. This is why when something is unknown, putting us into a state of confusion, our minds understand it as a threat. Confusion threatens our mastery of the world, and therefore we feel vulnerable. To compensate for this feeling of vulnerability, our brains crave answers to fix the confusion, and the fastest and easiest way to find those answers is when it's found with little or no thought. This is usually done by assessing a situation and then, as is commonly called, "jumping to conclusions."

When a person jumps to conclusions, they skip over thinking of multiple possible causes of a problem, and focus only on one, without sufficient evidence to back up that answer. By jumping to conclusions, you are in essence putting all of your eggs in one basket, and taking a risk; you hope your answer is correct, but really your chances of being correct lie in luck's hands. This is why your mind has an unknown box, the concept of abnormality; instead of juggling the confusion, it sets it down while it figures out which category to place it in.

Imagine taking a steaming hot tray out of the oven with your bear hands. Your brain senses the pain and discomfort caused by the searing heat of the tray, and you instinctively place it on the kitchen counter right beside. While you recover from the discomfort, you can find a permanent place for the tray. The cause of abnormality is that many people do not end up categorizing the "abnormal" object, and leave it out on their kitchen counter indefinitely. Similar to leaving a hot object out on your kitchen counter for too long, leaving something, or someone, in your abnormal box can cause damage to your own perception, to the glasses through which you see the world.

Instead of undoing the wires that make us label things as abnormal, we can use them to stimulate curiosity and create a drive to find answers. We have used this method of using a negative human instinct for the positive before, when we had discussed anger and emotions. We do not necessarily need to eliminate this aspect of human nature, rather we just need to learn how to use it.

Imagine the following scenario: you're a college student at a house party, and as you're making conversation with your friends, you notice somebody walk in. This person seems to be about fifty years old, is wearing a blue uniform, and shoves his way through the dancing crowd. He walks down to the basement, and you hear him yelling "Crazy hooligans! Go home!" At first sight, you definitely see this person as abnormal. Maybe this man is coming to the party, but who would invite an older man to a college party? You may try to place him in the worker category, but then why would he be screaming? Could he be mentally unstable? If so, why was he wearing a uniform? All of these attempts to fit the man into a category happen within a split second, and you decide to put it in the abnormal category until further notice.

At this point in the scenario, the road diverges into two paths. On the first path, the one most people take, you have the option of leaving the man in the abnormal box, along with everything else your mind tells you is "weird." This path will lead you to avoidance, and your mind tells you to avoid the abnormal object or person. On the second path, the one Robert Frost would call "the one less travelled by," you can use the confusion as fuel to drive your curiosity. You can ask the host of the party who that person was. When he tells you that he was his uncle coming over after work to pick up something from the basement, and was upset that his nephew threw a party without his parent's approval, the fog in your mind clears; you now understand the situation more clearly. Once you make meaning of the situation, your mind can remove the host's uncle from the "abnormal" box and place it in the box that contains "upset family members."

By taking the second path, several things occur. First, you give your mind clarity of a situation, thus mastering your environment. The first path would have given you the illusion that you are mastering your environment, that you at least placed the situation in a box, even though that box isn't meant to be the uncle's permanent destination. In reality, you would not have had full mastery and understanding of the situation until you have found a category other than the "abnormality" to place it in. Second, you don't jump to conclusions about the man himself. What if this man walked back upstairs and started interrogating you about the party and what the party's attendees were doing there? If you would have taken the first path, you might run away, answer fiercely, or make the man feel bad by embarrassing him for being "weird." Because you have taken the second path, however, you understand that the uncle is just concerned for his nephew and fears that somebody will get in trouble on the nephew's expense. Third, you are able to build a better understanding of the world for future events, thus changing the shape of your perception glasses permanently. This event, although occurring just moments ago, becomes a part of your personal experience. Personal experience, as we have said before, is one of the two ways people understand normality, therefore this experience permanently shapes your understanding of the world. Next time you encounter a situation such as the one you have just encountered, your mind will have a new category for convenient use, the "upset uncle" category.

So you've learned how to not jump to conclusions, but, as you're probably thinking, isn't this chapter about judgment? If you're thinking such, you're correct. However, as we've described previously, jumping to conclusions is the easiest way to get answers to the confusing world around us. Judgment comes in after you find the answers. Once you have your answers, whether they be incorrect and based on a flawed perspective or correct and by thoroughly thinking about the situation at hand, you evaluate it in your mind and assign it labels such as good or bad, fair or unfair, and so on. Based on this, we can say that there are two ways from which your judgment could be flawed: either you have a problem deducing the correct answers from a confusing situation, or you have a problem interpreting the answer as positive or negative.

We have already described how one can

encounter troubles when not finding the right answers, by jumping to conclusions, to something their minds understand as abnormal and confusing. Now, we move on to the second way of judging something or someone wrongly, at the evaluation step. Going back to the beginning of this chapter, your evaluation of something is largely dependent on a person's personal experience and on their respective societal standards. For example, if you love bacon and eat it with your breakfast every Sunday morning, your cheat day from your diet, you may evaluate bacon very positively. If, on the other hand, you live in a religious society where pork is not allowed, or the first time you tried bacon it was cooked very unwell, you may associate bacon with negativity, and evaluate it as such. The key word above is *association*, relating two concepts in your mind.

Association is closely related to categorization; categorization is the formation of boxes we place incoming information in, and association is the way we learn how to place each piece of incoming information in the box it belongs to. To take the table example again, when you see a new table, your brain finds similar characteristics it has to objects already in the "table" category, and therefore associates the new table with the older ones. This recognition of the similarity of a new stimulus with those already placed in categories is what association is all about. When a stimulus is so new that it cannot be related to anything you have previously experienced, your brain becomes confused and places the object in the abnormal category, as we have already explained.

Associations, as with other parts of human nature, can be controlled. Your mind naturally creates associations between similar objects, and people, however these associations are malleable; they can be molded to your liking when given enough diligence. One object can have many associations, however once a new object is associated with another, which happens instantaneously, it can never go back to being unassociated. In other words, once your mind has an association between a new object and an old one, the only way you can overcome that association is by replacing that association with a new one or by giving extra emphasis to its other associations.

To give an example, imagine you're the first human landing on Mars. As you descend from your spaceship, you look around and see a world of new objects you've never before encountered. A minute after you take your first steps on the strange planet, you take notice of a strange creature running up to you. The creature is big, green, and has three eyes. It has its gaze fixated on you, its arms, or at least what seem to be arms, are flailing around, and it's shouting something that you cannot understand. Take a step back now, and analyze what's going on here. There are several characteristics that you can attribute to this thing: it looks like it's alive, it's running, and it's screaming what sounds like gibberish to you. Your mind takes these characteristics, and recognize a similarity between this new experience and a previous one: that time when you were seven years old and your uncle's dog chased you. Your mind uses this association and places the creature in the "wild animal" and the "attacking" categories.

When the dog chased you, the child version of yourself attributed, or judged, it as negative because you did not like the fear it elicited in you. Now, many years later, your mind still understands wild animals running towards you as negative. When you associated this creature with a wild animal, you elicited that same fear in yourself, and judge the situation as negative, with a potential for harm. In response, you may run back to your spaceship, hide, contact Earth, and so on, in order to protect yourself from the threat.

Now, let's return to the scenario. You're standing by your aircraft and see this creature running towards you. Let's say that for one reason or another you do not run away and remain where you are. The creature runs up to you, hands you a tiny piece of technology, and uses hand gestures to instruct you to place the new tech in your ears. You do as it says, and suddenly you can understand what the creature is saying. The creature was running to greet you and welcome you to its planet. It tells you that it, and its fellow Martians, have been keeping an eye on Earth and have been anticipating this historic day for a long time. The Martian invites you to a lavish meal of both Martian and Earthling food, and a massive celebration occurs. You now take notice that these Martians are extremely friendly and hospitable, and create a new association. This association is between the Martians and your grandmother back at home, whom always loved inviting your large family over for dinner. While you now judge these creatures as much kinder beings rather than hostile animals, your mind still feels conflicted. This is because the two associations oppose one another, given that they are practically opposites, and you cannot associate the categories themselves. You have two opposite associations which contradict each other, so you can't keep them both. By giving emphasis to the kind and hospitable category, you can overcome the wild animal association to a point that it becomes negligible. You can also give emphasis to the positive association by spending more time observing and thinking positively towards the Martians, and spending little to no time with the negative association you've now deemed as inappropriate.

This process of losing associations that aren't being used occurs naturally, and in the brain this is called *synaptic pruning*. Synapses are the connections brain cells called neurons make with one another in order to transfer and maintain information. When information being maintained in a synapse isn't being used, and thus isn't being strengthened, that synapse eventually gets "pruned," and disappears, along with the information it contained. This is the same reason we do not remember insignificant information that has occurred in the past, such as what we had for breakfast on Thursday, four months and three weeks ago.

The key to good judgment is knowing how to take advantage of your associations. It's always good to be able to make negative associations, as long as those associations are made for the appropriate things. If a wild animal were to be chasing you, it would be beneficial for your mind to associate it with the dog that chased you when you were seven, that way you'd understand that you're in a dangerous situation and can act appropriately. However, if one of your siblings were to buy a puppy, it would be a disadvantage to fear the cute pet by associating it with the dog that had chased you so many years ago.

A good way to replace a bad association would be to create better associations by thinking of them. For example, you could think about a cute toddler every time your sibling's puppy is running around and playing. Every time you see the dog and begin to feel negative emotions, you can actively and consciously try to make the association between it and the image of a toddler. After time, you'll begin to grow more and more comfortable with the puppy, until you no longer have the negative emotions that were brought in with the wild animal association.

Another great way to not judge something wrongly, especially if that something is a person, is to actively be grateful for their existence. Being grateful implies finding a reason why that person's existence helps you, or how it can potentially help you. This is in essence the same as building positive associations, however here you're building them between the object and positive concepts rather than with other positive objects. We will return to the idea of gratefulness in Chapter Nine, however the basic idea of being grateful applies here as well.

When you judge something, especially when you do so openly, it effects your personality as well as your perception. If changing your perspective is like changing your glasses' prescription, judging would be like changing both the lens and their frames; not only is there a change in the way you see the world, but the world also notices a change in you. When you judge something for the good, you add a little color to the picture you're looking at, and vice versa to when you judge something negatively. Positive judgment makes the world seem to you a little brighter, while negative judgment does the opposite. Over time, by adopting positive thinking and getting rid of negative judgment, the world will become a much more beautiful place to live in. People who look up at life and make favorable judging a habit rather than an occasion are what we call optimists. When one thinks negatively and judges others unfavorably, they learn to not trust others and become pessimists. The more objects, and people, a person attributes positive and negative feelings to, the more objects and people he has to use for positive and negative associations respectively. When people are optimists or pessimists, the world takes note of it as character traits they demonstrate when they speak and give their opinion, and thus your own judgment processes shape the way others perceive you.

Judging becomes especially tricky when a

person is judging other people, because just as we tend to judge others instinctively, so do others towards us. Judgment becomes a triangle between ourselves (our own perception), others, and our personality; each one has an effect on the other two. When we judge someone unfavorably, we affect those we are judging by labelling them with a negative judgment, and affect our personality by giving us a negative outlook towards others. This in turn makes our perception of the world a bit darker. At the same time, our personality will affect the way we judge others in the future, and our personality will be taken into account when other people judge us. The same works for positive judgments.

Judgment, in essence, is more about yourself rather than about that which you are judging, and it is important to remember that when you feel yourself coming close to judging someone or something. While avoiding negative judgment may seem like a tedious task and an impossible goal to achieve, remember that this is already the seventh trait you are building to improve the quality of your life and your perception of the world. Every single one of the other traits we have discussed so far will naturally help you gain a brighter perspective and less judgmental mentality, so this chapter is really just a way of taking a hold of them and becoming consciously aware of their presence.

Challenge #7:

Before jumping to conclusions and judging

something or someone negatively, think about what your judgment says about you as a person, the consequences it can have on both yourself and that which you are judging, and if the judgment is justified.

Chapter 8: The True Self

"Be congruent. Be authentic. Be your true self." ~Mahatma Gandhi

Once upon a time there was a little boy named Jack. Jack belonged to a family of shepherds, and one day his family had decided that he was ready to watch the herd all by himself. Jack knew what his job entailed: he needed to make sure that no sheep get out of sight, and that no predators get into it. After ten minutes of shepherding, the family heard a shriek. "Wolf!" they heard Jack cry. Jack's eldest brother ran to help, however when he had arrived, he had discovered that there was no wolf in sight. "Jack," his older brother said, "you cannot yell for help unless you really need it." Everybody knows the rest of the story: Jack calls for unnecessary help several more times, until eventually he calls for help when it's truly needed and no help arrives.

What if Jack was anxious because of all the responsibility that came along with watching the sheep? The anxiety built up inside of him, and manifested itself as a wolf. This "wolf" was a way Jack was able to escape his fear, and cope with the anxiety; he called for help not to overcome a predator attacking the sheep, rather he called for help to overcome the fear attacking him, himself. The master of propaganda and making lies be believed, Adolf Hitler, had accurately described lies by saying "The victor will never be asked if he told

told the truth." Yes, Hitler was talking about victory over others and using propaganda in order to achieve that victory, however the same philosophy applies to individual thought. Jack used a lie as a vehicle to cope with his newly founded enemy, his anxiety, because he saw it as a way to be victorious. Yes, the lie may have allowed him to temporarily overcome his anxiety, however, as we saw in the story, it was only temporary. Once Jack's family learned that the wolf was just a faction of Jack's imagination, they returned him to his duty and Jack was stuck in his original problem again. If the result of lying is a temporary victory followed by a regression to a person's original problem, is it really a victory at all?

Many times, if a person repeats a lie enough, they will begin to believe it to be true themselves, even if they are the ones who had created the lie to begin with. This is so true, that if you were to hook them up to a lie detector, you would not detect the slightest sign of lying as they say what you both no is clearly not true. Children do this all the time; if you ask any school nurse, they will tell you that there are always some children whom complain of feeling sick every day, and every time the nurse calls the child's parents they are told the same thing: the child is anxious of the social scene of a classroom and will be at the nurse's office every day, even if they are not really sick. I can verify this from past experience, working at a summer day camp as the head of the camp's medical staff. While the child may be scared of the social pressure, and not actually feel sick, they will convince themselves that they are sick, enough that they will truly believe that they are feeling sick. If this is the case, are the children actually lying?

Lying and not speaking the truth entail two different things: in the first, one is consciously saying something untrue in order to deceive another, and the second is doing such in order to deceive themselves. When you lie to yourself, you are using your lies to avoid a feeling of uncomfortableness, one that comes from confronting a situation that comes from within. As we had explained in previous chapters, people tend to blame the external world for their inner problems, problems with their character traits or feelings, in what psychology calls the fundamental attribution error, a concept we will return to over and over throughout this book. This avoidance ends up working against you: only you know your true limitations, and those same limitations are set by none other than yourself, so avoidance ends up deterring you from finding your true potential.

So far in this chapter we have discovered a situation which arises from lying to oneself: on the one hand, lying does not lead to a permanent solution to one's problems, yet on the other hand the person may not be lying to begin with, because they believe in their lie wholeheartedly. In order to resolve this contradiction, we must restructure the way we define honesty and dishonesty.

Similarly to the term "lying," the term "honesty" means something different than the common understanding is. Many people understand honesty to be the opposite of lying; to them, being honest means telling the truth rather than telling a lie. In this chapter, however, we will look at honesty in a different light, and define honesty as transparency. Being transparent, as the term suggests, means that you have nothing to hide. The same way that you wouldn't hide something in a transparent bag, or hide from someone behind a glass window, being transparent in your character means not feeling ashamed in your actions and being fluent in your intentions. Telling the truth is not what makes a person honest, rather being honest leads someone to tell the truth.

Being fluent in your intentions means that when you act ,or think, a certain way, you know why you are acting or thinking as such and have clarity in your mindset. Jack, who wasn't fluent with his intentions, interpreted the imagined wolf to be a threat to the sheep rather than as an escape from his responsibility. If Jack were fluent in his intentions, however, he would have understood that screaming "Wolf!" would be a coping mechanism rather than a true call for help. This clarity would have ultimately had an effect on his decision, on whether or not he should call for help, because he would have understood that there is no true danger and a false alarm could have bad consequences for the future.

The second component of transparency, feeling ashamed of your actions, does not necessarily mean to be ashamed to discuss them in public. Many times, people are proud of their actions, however they will be hesitant to discuss them in certain settings for reasons such as privacy or appropriateness in that specific setting. Rather than being a public expression of your thoughts and actions, being ashamed of your actions is an inner feeling of rejection and regret towards your past actions. This feeling, an uneasiness of acting a certain way, can be predicted; before acting, one knows whether or not they will be proud of such actions. This knowledge is sometimes clouded by emotions and lying to oneself, depending on the situation at hand, however the clouds can be cleared with practice and recognition of ones belief of that action.

When you feel ashamed of your actions, you find excuses to validate them. For example, if somebody pickpocketed a person on the street, they will likely justify their robbery by claiming that the victim was more financially secure than them, and that they desperately needed the money. We all know that desperately needing money is no excuse for robbery, however, this excuse, a lie, is believed by the robber despite his knowledge that his actions are morally incorrect. His excuse creates a temporary victory over his moral insecurity, a temporary relief from the uncomfortable position, however, when it comes time to face the judge in court, he will evidently lose. Even if he is not caught by the police, "believing" that it is morally just for him to rob will lead him to rob again, and thus feel morally insecure again, to be followed with another excuse. This creates a cycle of wrongdoings and excuses, one that is difficult, yet not impossible, to break.

How ashamed one is of their actions and the level of their intention fluency are ultimately connected. The more one is ashamed of what they are doing, the more excuses they will make for themselves. These excuses cloud their understanding of their true intentions, and also perpetuate the cycle of acting in ways one is not fully proud of, in ays they are ashamed of. Their intentions change from "I desire money and don't care who I hurt in order to get it," or "I need to escape this stressful situation," to "Society has stacked the odds against me and I deserve the stolen money" and "There is a threat to me and my property." The opposite, however, occurs as well: if a person avoids creating excuses for themselves and begins to understand which actions they would be ashamed about, they will ultimately gain more fluency in their intentions when they act. The person will grow from excuses and acting unjustly to honesty and acting in ways that are beneficial.

When you think about the idea of excuses more carefully, a similarity arises between this chapter and the last; excuses are ultimately incorrect judgments of your own actions. To use the terminology of Chapter Seven, an excuse is a temporary box used to place the confusion of your actions. When you pick up the hot tray of the action, your mind feels the heat and pain and tells you to quickly put it down somewhere. For this reason, your mind creates an excuse to put it down on.

Excuses trick your mind into thinking that it has found a place for this action's confusion, however the location is incorrect and eventually it will be kicked out of that box just to become a confusion again.

In Chapter Seven we had discussed jumping to conclusions, but mostly discussed it in terms of jumping to conclusions about other people. If you shouldn't jump to conclusions about external things, even more so you should not jump to conclusions about yourself. As we had explained before, human nature is to assume that somebody else's actions were done due to their faulty character while we assume our own actions are a result of external forces, the fundamental attribution error. In order to rise above our human nature, we must flip the order: assume other people act as a result of external forces while our own actions are a result of our faulty character. By thinking this way, we can begin to judge others less, as we had learned in the previous chapter, and begin to see the flaws in our own character so that we can build on them.

One of the things people love to criticize politicians for is their lack of transparency. Politicians must know how to play the game of politics correctly in order for them to fulfill their promises to the people in the most efficient way so that they get reelected. However, with every game comes a way to cheat. Politicians may sometimes discover a way to handle a situation or make a profit, but in hidden and illegal ways, and are faced with the challenge of playing the game fairly or beating around the bush and cheating. Politicians who handle affairs slyly are what most people call "corrupt," and this is because they lack transparency. Instead of being open to the people they are meant to serve and represent, they are opaque and hidden.

Going back to our original question, how does transparency solve the problems of returning to one's original situation, such as Jack once his family realized he was lying about the Wolf, and of genuinely believing your lie? As we had explained before, being transparent means that you are fluent in your intentions and not ashamed of your actions, and that these two traits are intertwined. When you do not allow your human instinct to give you excuses for your actions, you become honest with yourself; when you mess up, you admit to your mistake rather than justify it, when you know you have a bad habit you work on it rather than give yourself excuses to continue it, and, most importantly, when you need to act you are able to differentiate between right and wrong, moral and immoral. When you become honest with yourself you have no reason to lie to others, because you know that lying will not fix any of your problems. By being transparent, you ultimately become honest, in the common sense of the term.

Lying, such as any action, is dependent on the circumstances; everyone can agree that lying to your spouse about an affair is immoral, however more complex situations become more controversial. Imagine that you are a German civilian in Nazi

Germany, and are hiding Jews in your basement, or that you are a Southerner in pre-Civil War America, and are hiding slaves in the Underground Railroad. Would lying in this situation be the wrong thing to do?

The reason that none of us would argue that lying in order to save innocent lives is the "wrong" thing to do is because you weigh the pros and cons of telling the lie; if you tell the truth, you would be giving up innocent lives to cruel murderers, and if you lie, you'd be saving them. In this situation, you would need to judge the action of lying in context of the situation, and you would deem it a positive action, because saving lives is better than taking them. If a person is transparent, they are free from the excuses distracting them from making correct decisions. They do not give themselves reasons to justify acting wrongly, and they are honest with themselves about what needs to be done and how it should be done. Now the question remains, how does one become transparent and, if you genuinely believe your lies to be true, how can you prevent them?

Yes, you do believe your lies when you lie to yourself, however there is still one fundamental difference between the real truth and the lie you believe to be true: while the first one is believed automatically, the second one is only believed after an initial step. To make this step a bit easier to understand, we can analyze it when the lie is coming from an external source and then apply it to when the lie comes from yourself.

There is a famous psychology experiment, called the Asch Paradigm, where a person is placed in a room with several other people and an instructor. The instructor shows the group of people an image of three lines of different lengths, and asks the members of the group one at a time which line is the longest. What the participant doesn't know, however, is that the other people are really actors, and were instructed to give the wrong answer. Instead of pointing to the longest line, they point to the middle-length line, that way they are obviously wrong, but not wrong enough that the participant has no choice but to argue. While they know that there is only one obviously correct answer, many times the participant will give the wrong answer in attempt to not look foolish in front of the others and to fit in. What happens here is very interesting: the participant notices that the other "participants" in the room, the actors, giving the actor the wrong answer, a lie, and a wave of confusion hits him. What happens a lot of times is that the participant is so confused, that he concludes that he is wrong and the others must be correct if they are all agreeing, and therefore believes in the lie himself. The social relief of fitting in rather than disagreeing with the group alleviates the pressure from him, and this is taken as a sign that he had placed the confusion in the right box, so his wrong answer must be the correct one (even though we all know this to be false).

This same step occurs when one is lying to themselves rather than believing an external lie. You find yourself in a situation where you know what the truth actually is, however the truth will put you in an unsettling situation. The situation can be moral insecurity, like the robber, or anxiety, like Jack. Your brain does not understand what it needs to do to in order to feel comfortable again, and it resides to believe in a lie to restore its comfort.

The only path to success is through hard work, and working hard is rarely comfortable. The key to success is learning how to be comfortable with the discomfort, to be transparent and confront your discomfort, and to use it as a trail marker on the hike to success. Get comfortable at using the discomfort of the truth in order to build character, and the only way to get comfortable with discomfort is to be honest and transparent with yourself.

Challenge #8:

Become transparent with yourself; accept your mistakes and character faults rather than excusing them.

Chapter 9: Thankfully So

"The man who says he can, and the man who says he can't. Are both correct.
~Confucius

You're stressed. You're a full time college student, hold two jobs, have three papers due by the end of the week, finals to study for, which happen to begin next Monday, still haven't confirmed your family vacation, and already wake up every morning at 5:00 AM just to fit it all into your schedule. You feel like the world is resting upon your shoulders, and you start feeling the stress have an effect on your physical and mental health. Then one day, out of nowhere, snap. You can't handle the stress, and you just crumble from the pressure. You're tired of the work, tired of the stress, tired of keeping up.

This was my life just a few months ago. I had a too many responsibilities that required my attention, and not enough hours in my day. When I arrived at work that afternoon, I told one of my coworkers about how I was feeling that day. She looked at me, and all she said was, "Pray." She elaborated and said that she doesn't mean to read verses from a prayer book. She said that I needed to speak to God, and make sure it came from the heart. I jokingly replied that I had already left God a voicemail, and that I'm still waiting for Him to call back. Later that night, however, I thought about it and realized something-it isn't I who left the message and is waiting for a call back from God, rather my life is full of so many great things that I take for granted, things I should be thankful for.

You don't have to be a person of faith to connect with this anecdote. Being grateful for what you have can be directed towards your family, friends, self, or towards a divine power. Sure, we have a lot of things that make our lives go up and down, but how fun would a rollercoaster be if it didn't have bumps, hills, and loops?

Instead of letting life's stressors put you down, use the things you are grateful for as tools to overcome them. Stress is all in your brain; it isn't an external force pushing inwards, rather it's your inner force not pushing outwards. Rather than letting the stress put you down, use the stress to put you up, and you can achieve great things.

Being honest with yourself is more than just accepting your faults and avoiding excuses, it's about making your words sacred and understanding the value in the world around you. Being fluent in your intentions and not being ashamed of your actions also includes future intentions and actions. When you set a goal and tell yourself that you want to achieve something, your words become set in stone.

There are times when you set a goal, but information acquired after they are set deter you from achieving them. This doesn't take away from your transparency, and all it means is that you know how to adapt your life and the goals you set in order to maintain your transparency; new information can change your intentions and how you feel about an action, thereby changing your ultimate plan. By setting your goals in stone, you increase your honesty because you deter yourself from making excuses. The more persistent you are in achieving your goals, the less likely you are to create excuses.

Today's world places more emphasis on productivity than ever before, and many people spend their entire lives trying to be as productive as possible in search for happiness. Unfortunately, too many people don't know how to be productive, and they never end up finding true happiness or fulfillment. Other people, who are harder to find, only see happiness and fulfillment. The difference between the two is that the second set of people understand that happiness isn't something you can find or chase after, rather it's something you must create for yourself.

Setting goals is important, however how you set them and however many you set is even more important. Setting goals that you aren't passionate about, taking them upon yourself without giving them ample thought first, or taking on too many commitments without enough time are all ways your goals can backfire on you.

There is a famous parable that goes as such: imagine every morning you wake up with a deposit of $86,400 dollars in your bank account. You can do whatever you want with the money, no strings attached. However, there's one limitation to this gift: you are not allowed to save the money you get, and once the day is over, every dollar you haven't spent is forfeited. Think over this scenario, and contemplate what you would do with the money. Surely you would try to buy as many things as possible .

Every 24 hours contain precisely 86,400 seconds. We can spend them to their fullest potential, using every single second, or we can waste them away, never to be regained. This is the challenge of productivity. Productivity is spending your time and resources to obtain the most value you can. Value, however, is a subjective term, and what is valuable to one individual may not be to another. It is up to each person to determine what and how much of it is of value to them, and the more you value your time, the more wisely you will use it.

Spending money is very much like spending time; wasting it is a shame, however it's worth buying few valuable and useful tools over buying many tiny and useless toys. In simpler terms, it is better to buy three cars than to buy 100,000 car fresheners. On the other hand, it may be better to buy several valuable, but smaller, objects than throwing all of your eggs into one basket. For example, it's smarter to buy several stocks in multiple companies rather than investing a lot in just one company. The best way to use your money, and time, wisely, is to not reach either extreme, overuse and wastefulness, and to find a balance between the two.

Learning how to not put all of your eggs in one basket is analogous to a child learning the concept of numbers. Child development consists of learning and developing new skills in order to live in the complex world we know, and one of these skills is the ability to differentiate between number and amount. For example, up until a child's toddler years, the child would not be able to understand the difference between two and two halves; if you were to give the child a cookie and they were to ask for another, you could easily break the cookie in half and easily get away with deceiving them. The child would be satisfied that they now have two cookies, even though they still have the same amount of "cookie." Once the child learns to differentiate between number and amount, however, you would have a hard time tricking them, and you would have to decide between giving them an extra cookie or having an angry child to deal with.

The first type of time misuse is by overusing it, by buying the 100,000 car fresheners. Many times, life deals us multiple opportunities simultaneously, and we all think that we can handle it all. After all, the greatest and most able person to take on those opportunities is us, according to our human nature. That may sound selfish, but it's a reality of human nature we must accept. As explained earlier in this book, the only mind we truly understand is our own, and therefore we think highly of ourselves in comparison to those around us. However, just because overestimating our abilities is a part of human nature doesn't mean we can't rise above it.

As we've stated before, we take on opportunities because they seem enticing rather than based on whether or not we can handle them. We accept them without thoroughly thinking through our ability to manage them, along with our already hectic schedules. Some people have this challenge more than others, however everybody encounters it at one point or another during their lifetime. The problem with taking on goals haphazardly is that we only have a limited amount of time and effort. Taking upon new opportunities, when we are already using our maximum time and effort, is in essence cutting the cookie into more pieces; just because you have more pieces doesn't mean that you are creating something new, nor are you being more productive. Instead of adding productivity, you are just rearranging your productivity by taking away from other responsibilities and adding it to a new commitment, a new responsibility. Responsibility, in this sense, can then be defined as something that requires your time and effort. How much time and effort you can contribute is therefore a consequence of how many responsibilities you must attend to.

The key to managing which responsibilities you take upon yourself, and how many you commit to, is prioritizing. When you prioritize, you create order to the chaos of commitments and goals you have. With prioritization, some responsibilities become consciously more important than others, and therefore you dedicate more time and effort to them. By focusing on your priorities, you are able to ensure that they receive enough time and effort needed to reach their full productivity potential. You also become aware of how much time you have on the side to devote to other goals of less importance as a result of prioritization. We all know which goals are of most importance to us, so prioritizing is just a matter of making the hierarchy of goal importance a part of our conscious rather than unconscious understanding. This can be done by thinking them through or writing them down on paper, depending on your preference.

The second extreme of time misuse is by wasting it, by letting the seconds of your day slip away from you, never to return. The definition of wasting time depends on the definition of productivity, which, to restate, is allocating your time and resources appropriately to things you find value in. To give an example, sleep would not be considered a waste of time because it is crucial for your health, however too much sleep is seen as a waste of time that can be used for other goal-oriented activities. Each person differs in how much sleep is valuable to them, however; some people only need four hours of sleep in order to stay healthy and function throughout the day, whereas others may need eight. How much value a person finds in something is dependent on their need as well as their perspective. Each person decides the value of something depending on the situation and their judgment of the situation.

Remember, we had started the chapter with gratefulness, and have somehow ended up discussing productivity. The two may seem to be two completely different topics, however they are just different players in the same field. Both productivity and gratefulness are ways of interacting with the concept of value, by obtaining the most value from life and appreciating the value you already have, respectively. Like any sport, each player is an individual of their own and is in control of their performance, however the other players in the game guide and influence their actions as well.

When you're grateful for something, or someone, you appreciate their presence as a part of your life, the key word being appreciation. Appreciation is a recognition of value, and if you take appreciation one step further, you get gratitude, the expression of appreciation.

A great way of training yourself to appreciate more is to work your way up from the bottom- when you begin to be grateful for the little things in life, the pleasures you will likely forget a short time after they occur, you will naturally begin to appreciate the larger things. The easiest method of being grateful for the little things is to actively recognize them every time they occur, to consciously recognize the bits of fortune that come your way. For example, if you happen to be running late to an important meeting, and on your way you drive easily through a busy intersection without any deterrence, take a second to reflect on how you are pleased that that small goodness just occurred. You can do this by verbally or mentally thanking the world for helping you out. Regardless of whether you define fortune as a divine power, the will of God, or as an event of natural causes, being thankful for it will have the same effect: you will begin to find value in your life events and find value in the time you have living that life.

Another way of training yourself to be grateful is by imagining life without the pleasure that had just occurred. You can do this by replaying the scenario in your mind without the pleasure, or, for those looking for a more active approach towards a reoccurring fortune, actually taking away that pleasure and living life without it for a period of time. This is the reason why somebody who eats ice cream every day will appreciate the next scoop of ice cream less than somebody who has just finished a three year diet. When you restrict yourself from a life pleasure, you find it to be of more value than when it is easily accessible, and become grateful towards it the next time it is presented to you. By appreciating and finding value of the fortunes that one has in life, a person can stop taking things for granted and start taking things for value.

Once you learn to appreciate something, you will begin to notice a drive to express that gratefulness towards it, gratitude. Gratitude, in essence, is how we return value to that which has added value to our lives; this is the reciprocity we have described in Chapters Three and Six. For example, a first grade student in elementary school who appreciates, and is therefor grateful for, their teacher's hard work may bring them a small gift one day to demonstrate their gratitude. The teacher will then appreciate the gift, and express gratitude by continuing to work hard, in an even more happy and diligent manner than prior to receiving the gift. This creates a cycle of gratitude and gratefulness, continuously adding to the value both parties find in one another.

This is very similar to the love described in Chapter Three, to reciprocity. In Chapter Three, we had explained that by doing random acts of kindness, even the most insignificant of actions, you will begin to develop love towards that you are acting kindly towards. Gratefulness does the same thing, however it defines value a bit differently than how love defines it. When you love something, the sense of value is geared towards that which is loved. In other words, you find value within the person or thing, and wish only the best for them, because you want their success and happiness. When you are grateful for something, you find value of that thing in your own life, and the sense of value is geared inwards, towards yourself. Another difference between love and gratefulness is that the sense of love is usually a product of the act of giving, while the act of gratitude tends to be a product of receiving. Both kindness and gratitude have the same ultimate effect, however: they both give you an understanding of value in those around you.

When you are grateful for every pleasure you enjoy in the world, you begin to see a more positive and happy world than the one you had lived in yesterday. To use judgment to explain this, recall the metaphor of judgment to color vision. When you are grateful towards something, you understand its value in your life and judge it more favorably and more fairly, adding a little more color to your perspective. The opposite effect occurs when you reject the value or prohibit yourself from appreciating something. You will ultimately judge the person or object unfavorably and with more bias, and your perspective of the world will begin to lose color.

To take gratefulness one step further and tie it back to stress, we can expand gratefulness to the misfortunes we experience in life. There is a famous saying that my father once taught me as I was growing up, and that is that one should be grateful for the bad that happens in his life as they are for the good. Recall how in Chapter Two our discussion of misfortunes, and how fear of misfortune is really just fear of the unknown. When you live life with the understanding that what seems to be your greatest curse may very well be your greatest blessing, you begin to look at misfortunes in a neutral light rather than a negative one. Once you learn to not handle misfortunes as negative experiences, you can begin teaching yourself to handle them as positive ones. Every negative experience has the potential to be your greatest blessing, and that fact in itself is something to be grateful for. As the Dalai Lama had once said, "Remember that sometimes not getting what you want is a wonderful stroke of luck."

Appreciating the negatives in life has two consequences: it helps you appreciate the positive even more, and it helps you achieve your goals by preventing stress. The first consequence is obvious: if you are grateful for negative experiences, even more so will you be grateful for positive experiences. The second one, however, is a bit less so. When you are grateful for the negative events in your life, they become challenges rather than obstacles. The difference between the two is that a challenge is meant to get your heart pumping and your mind focused on overcoming it, while an obstacle is meant to deter you from your path; challenges always have a path that leads to success, and just make its path a little uneven, while obstacles are meant to be blocks, cutting off access to the path itself. Changing life events from obstacles to challenges is the key to success; challenges are games meant to win, and they are games meant for you to be the victor.

Some challenges are harder than others, that is no doubt, however there are no obstacles which are impossible to overcome. In other words, there are no obstacles which cannot be turned into challenges. There is only one method that works in overcoming hard challenges, and it is summarized perfectly by the famous quote, said anonymously, "When a child learns to walk and falls down 50 times, he never thinks to himself: 'maybe this isn't for me.'" This is the true definition of persistence, one where giving up is not an option.

Most people think of persistence only as the

opposite of giving up, however persistence includes more than just that. Persistence is having your eyes focused on a goal, and never using the words "maybe this isn't for me" as an excuse for giving up. Many people think that if you don't give up you are persistent, even if your pursuit at success is one that is aimless- you have no clear strategy. Struggling aimlessly is not persistence, because persistence has an end goal, a destination. An identifying characteristic of persistence is when a person changes their strategy to attain a goal. The moment you need to change your strategy is the same moment in which you have the greatest excuse for giving up. When you avoided the excuse and are fluent in your intentions, you become persistent in your goal, in the path to success.

There is a psychological phenomenon termed the Self-Fulfilling Prophecy. This phenomenon describes a situation where a person's own belief about themselves causes them to act a certain way. Imagine you wake up in a good mood one morning, and, as you are getting out of bed, you told yourself "today is going to be a good day, I can feel it." This may cause your mood to be a positive one, thus granting you a good day. In reality, the only reason your "prophecy"□ came true is because stating it to begin with had caused it to come into being. If you would not have said that you believe today will be a good day, the day may very well have not been a memorable one.

The same works for saying the words "maybe this isn't for me." Many times we reach a challenge and are intimidated by it. By saying that the challenge is too overbearing, or that it is impossible to be overcome, we cause ourselves to not overcome it. When you notice yourself giving up, try saying the phrase "I will overcome this challenge, and I will be successful." When you tell yourself that you will be successful, you are doing the opposite of giving up- you are causing yourself to be successful and overcome the challenges that you face.

Saying that a challenge is "impossible" to be overcome is a paradox. In other words, stating that something is impossible is impossible in itself. The same way that fearing misfortune is really just fearing the unknown, saying that something is impossible just means that the way to overcome it is unknown. If you were to show somebody in the fifteenth century a picture of a car, and told them that in a few centuries this machine will be all over the world and used by millions of people, they would tell you that it is impossible. If you were to tell somebody in 1950 that in under 20 years the first man will walk on the moon, they would call you crazy. Impossibility is in the eyes of the beholder, and is a subjective understanding of possibility. The only time overcoming a challenge is truly impossible is when it is subjectively so, when you tell yourself that it is impossible. As Confucius once said, "The man who says he can, and the man who says he can't. Are both correct."

Challenge #9:

Next time you have a desirable opportunity ahead of you, double check if you can handle it and be the most successful you can be. Also notice the small pleasures in life, and be grateful for their existence. When given the chance, express gratitude for them, and you will see the world in a new light. But, most importantly, never give up.

Chapter 10: The Respectful Self

"The true mark of professionalism is the ability to respect everyone else for their styles and always find something positive in every dining experience and highlight it in your thoughts and words."
~Johnny Luzzini

Do you recall how in Chapter Four we've mentioned that every mind is equally complex, and therefore we are all equal? Well, to expand on that fact, if everyone is equal, then it only makes sense that everybody should be treated equally as well. You may be asking why this chapter is included here, and why does such an obvious concept need explaining. before answering this question, let's delve into the what it really means to respect.

The concept of respecting and treating people equally is found in many religions, and is even considered pillars and foundations for many of them. There is a famous anecdote told over in Judaism, in which one man approached the famous rabbi, Rabbi Akiva, and tried to surprise him with a difficult question. The man requested that the rabbi recite the entire Bible while standing on one leg. As the story goes, Rabbi Akiva stood up on one leg, and simply said the words "Love your friend as you love yourself," equating this one phrase to the entirety of the Holy Scripture and Jewish Law. In Christianity, it is also believed that Jesus once said the famous line, "Thou shalt love thy neighbor as thyself," and equated loving and respecting one's friend to loving God. Same goes for Islam, where loving and treating others is considered by many the "Golden Rule of Love."

Respecting others is pretty much common sense, however, unfortunately, many people do not abide by it wholeheartedly. As described multiple times before, we tend to give ourselves more leeway when we fault, and judge others harshly when they do. For example, if someone cuts you off when you're driving on the highway, you may honk your horn and begin a fit of road rage directed towards that person. Of course, as you would probably think, that person is stupid, has no respect for others, deserves to die in a car accident, etc. However, imagine that now you're at work and receive a phone call that your wife has just went into labor and is about to deliver your first child. As most people would, you run out of the office, hop in your car, and speed away to meet your pregnant wife at the hospital. As you're driving on the highway, you cut off one car in front of you because they're driving a bit slower than you need them to. Because you know that you must cut that person off in order to be present at the birthing of your child, the child that will make you a father, you do not think much of the action. On the other hand, the driver in the car behind you, who does not think he is driving slowly at all nor does he know about your situation, thinks of your action as disrespectful.

In both situations one driver is cutting off the other, however, in the first situation, you judge the reckless driver as a lunatic who, as some may even think, deserves to die in a car crash, while in the second you are doing what is just and expected of you. The problem here is that each driver only knows their own perspective of the situation, and they have no way of knowing what the other driver is thinking. Their focus is narrowed on the information they can obtain from their own observations, and each individual does not have enough information in order to make a conclusive judgment. The same goes for any other situation; you are judging the situation from your own mind's understanding, and there is no way of understanding how the other person understands the situation. Even if the other person explicitly tells you how they've perceived a situation, you still have a tendency to lean towards your own perceptions and conclusions. This is called bias, and this is the same reason why we generally prefer to have third party sources, such as a jury in a courtroom, judge a situation.

The first way to overcome bias is simple: you're doing it by reading this chapter. Once you understand that you're judging a situation from your own subjective observations rather than objective truth, you will think more before jumping to conclusions. You will also develop an understanding that there is more information about a situation that you don't have full understanding of, and therefore will give others the benefit of the doubt. If you are missing information due to your individual perspective, they are probably missing some information too, which is very likely to be the reason for your disagreement. How can you treat somebody disrespectfully, now that you have this understanding? Maybe the situation you're in is just a matter of lacking information, in which constructive conversation rather than confrontational arguing may be your best bet to resolve it successfully. Disrespect comes from action before contemplating and taking this into account.

Another way to overcome bias is by giving the other party the benefit of the doubt, a product of understanding that the other person may be missing information. A previous professor of mine at Brooklyn College used to say that whenever she would drive and somebody would cut her off, the same situation we've seen above, she would tell herself that maybe they had to use the restroom. Now that you can understand that they may have a valid reason for cutting you off, such as rushing to find a restroom, you begin to understand that their actions are not necessarily of bad intent. Once the thought that they may be acting in accordance to your own moral rules comes into play, and that you would act the same in such a situation, you can begin respecting their actions and thought processes. If this is the case for situations in which somebody acts against our understanding, even the more so we should respect others when their decisions are not of controversial matters. This chapter is similar to the forgiving of Chapter Four, in the sense that we do not understand others' perspectives, however respecting others expands to include all forms of interactions, not only when one person has faulted another.

All respect really entails is recognizing another's rights to be human and to act as you would expect yourself to act. If this is the case, it only makes sense to treat others as you would hope to be treated. This is a great trick to help teach yourself to respect others. Every time you're about to interact with another person, take a second to think whether or not you would be contempt if that other person treated you the same way. If the answer to that question is a blaring yes, then you should proceed as planned. If it's a no, however, you need to rethink how you were planning on acting, keeping in mind that other person will probably judge the situation, and yourself, from their point of view. If you know that you must criticize them, and that you will not make them satisfied no matter how you do it, a good way to proceed is by thinking which way of criticizing them will make them the least angry and the most likely to receive the criticism.

Put yourself in the other person's shoes-treating people with respect is not only about how you would hope to be treated. True, thinking about how you would hope to be treated is a great start, however it is only a beginning step towards full respect and equality. This level of respect is the only one you can reach when interacting with an unfamiliar face, a stranger. When you're dealing with somebody you know, a family member or a friend, you can surpass this level and begin to not only consider how you yourself would like to be treated, rather also how they would like to be treated. The closer you are to somebody, the more you understand their character traits, perceptions, and preferences. These may differ from your own character traits, perceptions, and preferences, however, and understanding their own reactions and attitudes to how people interact with them allows you to access parts of their mind and understand their side of the story. You can never fully understand how a person's mind works, but the better you know them, the closer you can get to that unobtainable understanding.

This chapter was intentionally placed after the chapters on honesty, achieving your goals, and gratefulness. This is because you can now understand the mechanisms of understanding how you would like to be treated, and what you have to gain by being respectful towards others. In order to know how you would treat yourself, you must be transparent. A common excuse heard from people who act disrespectfully, criticize harshly, etc. is that they would be fine if someone were to act that way towards them. The problem here is that they are observing their actions from a subjective experience, and giving themselves leeway by claiming that they would have appreciated the same reaction towards themselves. If you become transparent, however, and are fluent in your intentions, you will see that your disrespect is more of a way to rid your emotions rather than solving a problem. When you walk through life with respect for those around you, you will achieve your goals much more successfully, and you will now have the support of others around you. In contrast, when you are disrespectful, you will have a much harder time gaining the support and advantages others can provide, advantages that will be happily given to you were you a respectful and considerate person towards others. Once you live life with others backing you up, you will have much more to be grateful for, and many people to make your world perspective more colorful. More people will act kindly towards you, more people to whom you would want to show gratitude and return the favor by being even more respectful and kind, or even by providing them with advantages when you can. While the above may seem unrealistic, or idealistic, that is because this is a lifestyle choice rather than a one-by-one sequence of actions. This lifestyle takes time to develop, and is something you will only see after years and years of practice. But, as the old Chinese proverb goes, "The best time to plant a tree was 20 years ago. The second best time is now."

A common theme that we've mentioned throughout the past chapters is that the way you act towards the world is usually the way the world will act towards you. We've mentioned this when it comes to acting kindly towards others and when judging others positively. When respecting others, the world and its inhabitants will act the same way, and respect you for it. Imagine you are observing a heated argument, and one participant is yelling and being disrespectful and the other is replying calmly and respectfully. I'm sure the second you read that sentence you had already assumed that the one speaking calmly and respectfully was the correct one in the argument. The second somebody becomes disrespectful, they lose all credibility in their opinions. Think about it, would you trust that somebody who doesn't have the decency to act respectfully ? Would they be the right person whose opinions you should follow wholeheartedly?

The reason why the above scenario is so rare is because people sense tension levels in every interaction. If one person is acting or speaking disrespectfully, their counterpart will feel the tension in the interaction rising, and will probably reciprocate as such. If the opposite occurs, however, and one of the participants is acting respectfully, as one should, this will also be reciprocated. Yes, you can always find people that break this rule and will act disrespectfully in the face of respect, however you are reading this book with the intent to do the same. By acting respectfully in the face of disrespect, you are breaking the commonality of human nature. The same goes for a respectful personality, where people will naturally treat respectful people with respect, and will naturally be hostile towards hostile counterparts. The principle here is simple: the more you treat others respectfully, the more you will be respected.

Challenge #10:

Before you act, speak, or even think

about others, think about how you would appreciate it if it were the other way around, and you were the one being acted towards. Treat everybody the way you would like for yourself, and turn respect into a lifestyle rather than a single action.

Chapter 11: Mindful Reactions

"A moment of Patience in a moment of Anger saves a thousand moments of Regret."
~Ali Ibn Abu Talib

We live in a world of reactions; we react to people interacting with us, we react to the weather outside, we react to the news, etc. A reaction is an action someone takes in response to something external, whether it be conscious or unconscious, by choice or habit. Reactions are how we live our lives, are part of our human nature, and are what shape us into the people we are today.

Like any other part of human nature, reactions can be controlled. Yes, we must react to everything, however how and when to react is completely in our control. The following chapter could be argued to be the most pinnacle of this book, because taking control of your reactions is the summation of the previous ten chapters (specifically Chapters Five through Ten, all of which attempt to help you take control of and shape your reactions). This chapter also marks an important transition, from trying to take control of your inner beliefs and thought processes to controlling your external interactions with the world. Up until now, every chapter described the average person's thoughts and perspective of what goes on around them, but now we will describe the appropriateness of taking actions that the world will see and remember you for.

As said before, controlling your reactions consists of two parts: *how* and *when* you react. The how part consists of the best methods of reacting to something, whereas the when part is the timing which will provide you with the best and most appropriate reaction.

In the last chapter, we've mentioned that giving people the benefit of the doubt is a useful tool for respecting others. By giving people the benefit of the doubt, you are in essence telling yourself that maybe the other person could not help acting the way that they are, and that maybe they had an understandable reason for being forced to act that way. In contrast, this chapter includes the times when you cannot give people of the doubt, when the person could and should have acted differently. The type of respect we focused on last chapter was the respect of not reacting, however now we will discuss the times to react and how to do so, both respectfully and successfully.

The types of reactions we will focus on here are those that you can control. Reactions that you cannot control, such as shivering in the cold or pupils constricting in the dark, are of no use here because those are not the type of reactions that will impact our character traits and interpersonal relationships; if everybody does something and it isn't bad, then it cannot shape us differently than it will to others. The type of reactions that will matter the most here are those that are a result of other people's actions- reacting to reactions.

Deciding when to react is the first step in reacting successfully; when is it appropriate to react and when is it not? To return to the idea of giving people the benefit of the doubt, the mere fact that there is a doubt is enough to give you the necessity to decide if you should react or not. Once you have even the smallest of doubts, there is the possibility of reacting in a way that will be unsuccessful or unnecessary, or both.

To use the same metaphor as Chapter 10, imagine a car cut you off as you were driving on the highway. There is the doubt that maybe the other driver is rushing to the hospital, so reacting by honking or getting angry would be unnecessary. There are times, however, when you have a doubt, yet it would still be appropriate to react. To give an example, let's say you find a ten-year-old child that ran away from home. You can say that there is a possibility that the child ran away because he was being abused at home, a reason that makes his choice appropriate, however you would still need to react to this child because it would be unethical to leave the child alone on the streets.

There are two general rules when it comes to reacting based on doubt: first, if not reacting, assuming that the doubt is true, would have negative consequences, then you should react. Second, the more likely the doubt is to be true (if the first rule does not apply and not reacting would have positive consequences), the less likely you are to need to react.

So now you have determined, based on whether or not you can find a doubt, if you should react or not. If your answer was no, then you can ignore the situation- you should not react. If, however, you decided that reacting would be the best course of action, then you must move onto the second step of deciding when to react: will your reaction be based on emotions, or based on a well thought out plan?

Let's walk down Memory Lane, and take our minds back to Chapter Six. In Chapter Six we had discussed controlling your emotions, and how acting emotionally is synonymous to acting impulsively. When you act out of emotions, you are not thinking out your plans thoroughly, and therefore can act in way which will leave scars on yourself and those you are acting towards. Emotional reactions tend to be for the sake of reacting rather than for the sake of a goal. By reacting to somebody emotionally, you are hammering nails into them, nails which leave holes even if taken back. This is why it is important to recognize your emotions, and to recognize when they need not have an influence on your actions. Generally, you can recognize emotions if you feel an impulse to react; if you feel like reacting is necessary, then it is probably because your emotions are demanding a reaction rather than your own logical thinking.

If you can recognize that you are feeling emotional at any given moment, then you can recognize whether or not your reaction is necessary. The opposite is true, as well: just because you feel emotionally inclined to react does not necessarily mean that reacting is bad. All it means is that you need to reconsider *how* you will react. A good way of evaluating the necessity of a reaction based on emotions is to stop, and wait until your emotional state calms down to neutral, or close to neutral. Imagine, for instance, you younger sibling accidentally ran into you and knocked you over. If you become angry at them and feel the need to punch them, stop, and wait an hour or two (or until you don't feel angry anymore). Most likely you won't want to start a fight anymore, and therefore you know that your reaction was unnecessary in this situation. The same works with positive emotions. Imagine now that you have received a very expensive birthday gift from your boss. The moment you unwrap your present and recognize what they had gotten you, you may feel immense love towards your boss. Your emotional experience may tell you that the best way to express your gratefulness, to show gratitude, would be to run up to them and give them a hug. If you simply wait until that immediate feeling of appreciation washes over, you would probably recognize that jumping on your boss and giving them a hug would be an inappropriate reaction. A more proper reaction may be to write them a thank you letter, or take them for lunch on you during your next lunch break together. Be honest with yourself when you reflect on emotional experiences; be fluent in your intentions, by consciously understanding their source as emotional or logical, and make sure you will not be ashamed of your actions, by thinking them out thoroughly and with a clear mind.

The final step in understanding when to react is to determine the effect your reaction has on yourself and others. There are two things that determine the effect of your reaction: how your reaction is done, and how it is received. The reason this step is placed under the *when* rather than the *how* to react is because determining the effect of your reaction will determine whether or not you should react to begin with.

Before reacting, you must consider how the person on the receiving end of your reaction will accept it. Let's return to the speeding driver analogy. Imagine the driver cutting you off had accidentally crashed into you, and had created a significant dent in the back of your car. You both pull over, and the other driver, who you notice happens to be six-foot tall, muscular, and covered in tattoos, exits his car first. As he gets out of the vehicle, he slams the door and starts walking towards you with his hands balled into fists. Your best option here, given that you are obviously smaller and weaker than this person, would not be to exit your car and start yelling and cursing at him. If you were to do that, I'm sure you could only imagine how it would be received; not well, that's for sure. In this case, your best bet would probably be to not react, and allow the other driver to control the outcome of the situation.

Determining your reaction's effect can be done by strategizing, as we had explained back in Chapter Two. To reiterate what we had said, strategizing includes contemplating all of the possible courses of action, and judging their respective consequences. In your mind, or on paper, you can map out the reactions along with their effects, and analyze them as a whole. If your chances of being productive with your reaction, having a positive effect, are good, then you should progress. If not, however, then it may be time to reconsider reacting and consider leaving the situation alone. The key to knowing when to react is to determine whether or not you will end up in a better position than you were before your reaction- will your reaction change the situation for the better or for the worse?

Once you determine whether or not you should react, you must determine *how* you will react. For this you can use strategizing again. However, this time you must focus on which reactions will have which consequences. Once you determine this, you can decide which reaction to pursue.

Whenever you respond to something, it must be done with the intent to improve. Criticizing is useless while critiquing is key. The difference between the two is simple: criticism is meant to hurt, critique is meant to heal. When you react with the attempt to better the future, you react more productively. Emotional reactions tend to be aimed at hurting; they are a way to relieve emotional buildup within you, and for the sole purpose to do something rather than nothing. When you plan out your reactions before reacting, your specific reaction must be the one that will better the future the most. Ask yourself the following question before taking a course of action: will I be a better person, or will the situation improve, after I react the way I had planned to?

If you're the one on the receiving end of the reaction, all of the above applies. Take a second and imagine that you had made an error at work, and your boss is critiquing you for it. While your boss is critiquing you, consider to yourself that they are probably doing so in order to help you and the company you both work for. If you can tell that they are reacting emotionally, lead by example, and be the more superior person by not responding emotionally to their reaction. The saying goes "fight fire with fire," however only water can truly put a fire out. Instead of trying to put out a person's fire with more fire, using kindness and thought out reactions will be the water needed to end the flame.

In order to react towards somebody effectively, you must approach the situation with the mindset that the other person can build and overcome the fault that you are reacting towards. Highlight this last sentence in your mind. The same way you are reading this text with the intention of changing for the better, so too do those around you have the potential to improve. You must approach any situation as a leader: another person's fault is your fault, and their loss is yours. You react to their misfortunes with the intent to succeed, because their success is your success, because a pleasure for them is a pleasure for you.

Challenge #11:

Think before you act. Your reactions are the way you interact with the world, and they shape who you are and how the world sees you.

Chapter 12: Desiring the Undesirable

"The discipline of desire is the background of character."
~John Locke

Desire: it's the little voice inside your head nudging you towards that last piece of chocolate cake; the one that tells you to spend time with your significant other; the one that says not to cross the street when cars are passing by. It is the voice of our wants, and is the voice of our inner most human nature.

Desire is the way our body tells us what it thinks we should do. This doesn't mean, however, that it is always correct. Desire voices opinions rather than facts; sometimes you may desire what is good for you, such as going to the gym so you can get that summer body you've always dreamt of, and sometimes you may desire what is harmful for you, such as a fancy car you can't afford or a cigarette for somebody trying to quit smoking. The voice of desire is the voice that says "something is missing, fix it now," the key word being "now." *Now* implies that following your desire is an impulsive act, because you feel as if you need to fix what is missing immediately. Consequently, acting emotionally becomes following your desire to react, hence the description of acting through emotions as impulsivity.

Notice how desire voices the opinion of the body, not that of the mind. That is because our minds, unlike animals, have the ability of thinking beyond our feelings. The body tells you what it thinks it wants at a given moment, while the mind tells you what you need for the long term, to accomplish your goals. The mind also tells you what you want long term for yourself as well as for those around you, while the body is only interested with itself. This difference only exists, however, if the previous chapters have been incorporated into your life; your mind only knows what it needs to accomplish your long term goals if you are honest with yourself, it only knows what is true and necessary if you use your mind to think rationally, etc.

Our human nature is to go from desire to contentment- when you desire something, something that your body feels is missing, you wish to fulfill that which you desire and fill the emptiness your body tells you exists without it. This is why when babies want anything, their first reaction is to cry. Crying is an expression of extreme discomfort, whether it be physically or mentally, and for babies, who are still learning what is and is not a discomfort worth crying over, these discomforts are exaggerated. If babies are hungry, they'll cry, if they're tired, they'll cry, if their diaper is wet, they'll cry, etc. They learn that crying is a way they can express their discomfort, and that it will summon an adult to satisfy their desires. Desire is also the voice countering confusion; when your mind is confused, you desire to find a response to the confusing object or event, and thus place it in the "unknown box." Recall the analogy of picking up a hot tray and needing a place to put it down. Desire yells "I don't want to be burned, put down the tray!" It will feel satisfied by dropping the hot tray on the counter, and will tell you not to touch it again, even though you know placing the tray on the counter is only a temporary spot for it. Controlling your desire is then analogous to wearing oven mittens- controlling your emotions allows you to make the right choices and steadily handle the hot trays in your life.

Controlling desire is a learnt skill, similar to every other topic in this book. Overcoming your human nature as a whole is a learned process, the precise reason you decided to read this book, and there are two main ways learning can occur: classical and operant conditioning. In classical conditioning, the type of conditioning used to learn natural reflexes towards unnaturally an object that usually would not make someone respond is paired with another object that normally would. Using the famous example of Pavlov's experiment, imagine presenting a dog with food. When dogs are presented with food, they naturally salivate. If you ring a bell immediately before presenting the dog with food, after multiple trials the dog will begin to salivate in response to the ringing bell, even if no food is presented.

The second type of conditioning, operant conditioning, will be of more value to us in terms of desires. Operant conditioning uses punishment and reward as a basis for learning rather than a naturally response-eliciting object used in classical conditioning. You can think of operant conditioning as the way people teach children how to behave correctly. Imagine a child does not share their toys with their siblings. There are two ways you can teach your child how to behave properly and share their toys: you can either punish them, and send them to their room whenever they do not share, or you can reward them, and give them a piece of candy when they do share with their siblings. You can also do the opposite- if the child misbehaves, you can remove a previous reward they were receiving, such as taking away a video game they enjoy playing every day after school, or, if they do behave, you can take away a punishment they were already being punished with, such as giving them back the video game or allowing them to leave their room. Operant conditioning does not only apply to children, however; adults can learn behaviors via operant conditioning as well.

To take operant conditioning one step further, we can condition ourselves to behave and think however we would like to, and thus overcome desire's strength. We can even use operant conditioning as a tool to learn any other of the character traits we've discussed in this book. You may be asking at this point why conditioning is being presented now rather than in the beginning, and to that I would answer that before you receive the tool to overcome human nature, you must first be presented with a use for it. A man that is given a gun without being told that he must fight in war may end up robbing innocent people, or he may decide to become a police officer. Now that you have a direction to turn towards, a target to aim at, you can use the tools of conditioning and overcoming desire in order to overcome human nature and become your supernatural self.

Imagine that, for example, you have a strong desire to eat a piece of cake at your friend's birthday party, however you are on a strict calorie-counting diet and know that this cake will strictly deplete your calorie allowance for the rest of the day. The punishment of a decrease in calories you are allowed to consume deters you from following your desire. This is because, by having a desire to not be punished, you confuse the voice of desire to voice your true opinion. Yes, the voice of desire cries "I want cake," however it also says "I want enough calories to eat dinner tonight!" The same works for rewards- if you can find a way to healthy way to reward yourself for not behaving according to your desire, you can confuse your desire to behave in accordance of your own morals and needs. This only works, however, if the desire for the reward is stronger than your original desire. In other words, you must choose something that you know you will want more than the original desired object.

Desire is a slippery slope, and you may fail at times. It is important, therefore, to remember the skills you've learned over the course of this book to get back up and learn from your deviations. If you set a reward system for yourself, you reward yourself every time you do not succumb to desire, and fail once, ask yourself if your reward is large enough? Desire has a nifty trick it can play here, and sometimes you will catch yourself desiring to increase your reward. The reward you allow yourself to set must be at a healthy level, and overindulgence in any reward can become a desire you will need to overcome in the future. If you allow yourself too much reward, to the point that it becomes an unhealthy desire in and of itself, then there is no point in using a reward system at all. The inverse applies to punishment- if you follow your desire to decrease the punishment every time you act in accordance to your desire, eventually the punishment will become small enough that it loses its effect to deter you from desire.

To make this concept more clear, imagine you are on a diet again. You allow yourself a slice of a chocolate cake every evening, on the condition that you have maintained your calorie count for the day. Several days after beginning this reward system, you receive a text at work from a group of friends inviting you to go out with them for dinner. As anyone who has ever dieted can tell you, it is nearly impossible to maintain a calorie count when you go out to eat. You decide that one night going out is okay, and you will choose the healthiest dish on the menu. Once at the restaurant, however, you realize that the healthiest option on the menu still exceeds your calorie count, and you have no other choice but to order an unhealthy dish. You enjoy the night, and at about midnight, you return home. After a full day of work and a night out, you are exhausted. As you head to bed, you pass by the kitchen, and you take notice of the chocolate cake sitting on the kitchen counter. You stop mid-stride. The room is dark, but there, under the spotlight of the only lit light bulb in the dark kitchen, you see the sparkling crumbs on the tray around that fudge brownie chocolate cake. You feel yourself beginning to salivate, and just as you stretch your hand out to grab the knife, you remember what you've had for dinner. "Eh," you think, "I'm allowed to mess up one day, I can still have the cake." After several times of not keeping to your diet but still having the cake, having the slice of cake at night becomes another desire, and a bad habit, deterring you from being healthy. You've begun your diet with the goal of destroying you unhealthy eating habits, and now you have unhealthy eating habits as well as a daily slice of chocolate cake before bed.

Before you can begin your struggle to overcome your desires and live a more fulfilling life, you must decide which desires must be overcome. We can all understand that some desires are not favorable, and therefore must be overcome, however is it possible that the concept of "desire," as a whole, an unfavorable trait? The answer is no, and, unsurprisingly, a balance must be found between helpful and harmful desires.

Somebody who cannot stray from his desires is called an addict. Such a person is enslaved to that which they desire, and feels compelled towards it to the point where they lose all control. The opposite of an addict would be a strong believer in Buddhism, or a Buddhist monk. Buddhist belief consists of the connection between desire and suffering and that, according to Buddhism, desire is the root of suffering. This is because Buddhism argues that desiring something that cannot be attained, such as immortality, can only cause suffering, and therefore all desires and attachments to the physical world is the source of suffering. These are two extremes, addicts and monks, and a healthy lifestyle is one which balances the two, a lifestyle that includes eradicating unhealthy desires while still maintaining those that make us human.

During my high school years I was fairly out of shape; I was not unhealthy, however I definitely could have used more physical activity. I had decided one day that I was going to begin going to the gym, and had hired for myself a personal trainer, we'll call him John, to help me get the hang of exercising properly. My one problem, as I had explained to John, was that I had a tendency to fall out of habits I did not enjoy, and fall into my desire to not exercise, even though I was very well aware of how much I had needed it to be in shape. John had given me one piece of advice which can be applied to every desire one tries to overcome: you must learn to love the pain. He explained that yes, lifting weights and being active is a strenuous experience, however, if I wanted to be the most efficient and get the most out of my gym membership, I needed to love the pain associated with the exercise.

What you like and dislike, what you desire and do not desire, is learned as you live your life. Even things which you would think are naturally disliked, such as the smell of rotten eggs or the pain of lifting weights, are learned by experiencing them first. Using conditioning, any dislike can become a like and vice versa, however it is up to you to take control of what you ultimately desire.

At the end of the day, living a healthy lifestyle isn't about overcoming what you desire, rather it's about taking control of what you desire. If you desire productivity and accomplishment, you will be productive and accomplish great things, and if you desire leadership and growth, you will grow into a leader you have a potential to be. You are the driver of your life, and life is the road in front of you. You can continue driving straight on the highway, driving steadily and easily forever, or you can follow your GPS through the bridges and tunnels, turns and exits, and end up at any destination you choose to aim for.

Challenge #12:

Choose one desire you currently have, one that you struggle with and is prevalent in your life, and use conditioning to overcome it. Choose one that is small, and once you feel it is overcome, move on to the bigger desires you wish to overcome.

Epilogue: The Final Step

"Life is like riding a bicycle. To keep your balance you must keep moving." ~Albert Einstein

Imagine yourself riding a bicycle along a path. The path contains twists and turns, hills and troughs, shade and sun. You turn left and right, pedal up and cruise down, change gears and steer. Riding a bicycle has many different components, but no matter which component you are currently focusing on, there is one thing that does not change during the entirety of the ride: you continue pedaling forward.

The key step, the foundations of being able to successfully live a life above human nature, is to leave the past in the past and live the future today. You can live in your failures, in the mistake of others, and in the desires of short-lived pleasures, or you can be honest with your intentions, think before you react, and desire a better future.

Nature is restricted by time, but people are not. Being above the restriction of time does not mean that you can time travel, rather being above time means that you, as a human being, can weigh the benefits and drawbacks of now with those of the future. Unlike animals, people have the ability to abstain from pleasures in the present in order to provide pleasures in the future. Animals, on the other hand, do not have a sense of the future. If you present a hungry animal with food, for example, it will eat it without considering how much food it will have available that night for dinner.

Being above time and living outside of the current comes with a challenge: you not only have an understanding of the concept of future, rather you also understand the concept of the past. We have the ability to commemorate past events and learn from past mistakes, however we can also allow the past to hold us back from living our full potential.

Time is like a tug-of-war game, with one side being the past, the other being the future, and the flag in the middle being the present. If you give too much strength to the past or to the future, you will not be able to live in a balanced present. By balancing the two, you are able to keep the flag centered and stable, ready to withstand pressures from any direction.

We must remember the past to repeat success in our future, and shape the future so we do not repeat the faults of our past. If you live in the past, the past will shape you, but if you live with the future in mind, you will shape the future.

The Ultimate Challenge, #13:

Keep your head in the future, and live your life by growing from the past- time can be your tool, or you can be a tool of time. By being above time's constraints, you can finally reach your supernatural self.

ABOUT THE AUTHOR

Moshe Shalom is a pre-med Brooklyn College student, studying Psychology, Biology. He has work experience in both the fields of medicine and education, both which require close human interaction as well as an understanding of the inner mechanisms the human mind.
With experience in poetry and inspirational writing, Moshe has a passion for helping those around him through creative writing, helping people reach their full potential and not underestimate their capabilities.

Made in the USA
Middletown, DE
16 May 2022

65841470R00090